JUDAISM AND WORLD ORDER

HUGH J. SCHONFIELD

*"And in the days of these kings shall the God of heaven
set up a kingdom, which shall never be destroyed."*

Daniel ii. 44

PREFACE

This is a Jewish War, say the Nazis. And many in the Democracies believe that there is a substratum of truth in this reiterated assertion. Because of it two million Jewish men, women, and children have been brutally exterminated, millions more have been tortured and starved. Before the sufferings of Israel the horror of Lidice pales into insignificance. It is doubtful whether much more than two-thirds of the Jewish people will survive the conflict.

It is high time, therefore, at least among the United Nations, that it should be understood what Judaism represents and what is its world outlook. Consequently in this little book I have been more outspoken than many Jews would care to be. But I have felt that what I had to say needed to be said at this time more than at any other. Judaism is so catholic that every Jew can place his own interpretation upon its fundamental doctrines; so that it will not invalidate anything I have written if some Jews do not agree with all of it. But I have certainly endeavoured in all that I have attributed to Judaism to give a collective view, and I have therefore drawn liberally on a variety of authorities, Jewish and Christian. It seemed to me that on such a subject what a man says in his own name would be more liable to criticism than what he can say in the name of others worthier than himself.

There is another reason for the book. It is intended to be a popular companion to several volumes on *Christianity and World Order*, by the Bishop of Chichester, and by others. It may thus, I hope not unworthily, contribute to the spiritual solution of some of the urgent and vexed problems of our day.

The final constructive section, where my personal convictions have principally intruded, will, I trust, help towards the creation of a common platform for the two great Bible Faiths, and by that much advance their progress towards that Kingdom of God on earth which is their joint conception of the only World Order built on everlasting foundations.

Since the body of this book was drafted there has been announced the formation in this country of a Council of Christians and Jews, with the highest spiritual dignitaries as Joint-Presidents. I regard this step as one of the most hopeful indications that a new era of mutual understanding is dawning, and by so much is the message of my volume reinforced. By permission I have given a statement of the Council's aims in Appendix B.

Since then, also, following upon the presentation of a Note by the Polish Government furnishing evidence of Hitler's policy to exterminate the Jews of Europe, there has been publicly delivered a Declaration by the United Nations on this subject (reproduced in Appendix C). The Declaration, approved by the Press and Public, has done something towards breaking what the Chief Rabbi has described as "a studied silence" on Jewish sufferings "unshaken by pronouncements of the Primate, of Cardinals and Archbishops who have all denounced this most appalling crime that the world has ever seen." But ignorance about the Jews and Judaism is still profound and widespread, and my small efforts at enlightenment appear therefore to be all the more timely and necessary.

HUGH J. SCHONFIELD.

London, *December* 1942.

Contents

PREFACE   3

PART ONE   9

The Message Of Universalism

Chapter I   11

The Source of New World Orders

Chapter II   21

What Is Judaism?

Chapter III   39

The Vision of the Prophets

Chapter IV   49

The Message of Judaism to The Ancient World

INTERVAL   61

The Great Test

PART TWO   69

Evangel for Nations

Chapter I   71

Anonymous Ben Anonymous

Chapter II   87

Negative Aspects

Chapter III   99

Has Judaism a Programme?

Chapter IV   109

The Holy Nation and World Order

Appendix A   **119**

World Benefactors of Jewish Faith or Heritage

Appendix B   **123**

Statement of Council of Christians and Jews

Appendix C   **127**

Treatment of Jews: United Nations' Declaration

PART ONE

The Message Of Universalism

"When the harp of Judah sounded, thrilled with the touch of inspiration Divine, among the echoes it waked in the human heart were those sweet sounds whose witcheries transport the soul into the realms of happiness. That melody has been our source of courage, our solace and our strength, and in all our wanderings we have sung it. It is the music of the Messianic age, the triumph-hymn to be one day thundered by all humanity, the real psalm of life as mankind shall sing it when Israel's world-task of teaching it shall have been accomplished. Its harmony is the harmony of the families of the earth, at last at peace, at last united in brotherhood, at last happy in their return to the One Great Father."— H. Pereira Mendes, 1887.

Chapter I

The Source of New World Orders

I

It is unfortunately inevitable that this book should begin with reference to a lie, for thousands have believed it, and too many do so still. Very largely because of it the horrors of this Second World War have fallen upon humanity. We have to expose this lie, but gladly shall we turn from such a distasteful negative duty to the positive task of presenting truth. The necessity is due to that perverted genius, Adolf Hitler, who has been the principal purveyor of the lie in question. He stated himself in his book *Mein Kampf* that "the very enormity of a lie contributes to its success.... The masses of the people easily succumb to it, as they cannot believe it possible that anyone should have the shameless audacity to invent such things.... Even if the clearest proof of its falsehood is forthcoming, something of the lie will nevertheless stick."

So, alas, it is. The lie in so many words is that the Jews are responsible for the War, and that it is part of their secret conspiracy to dominate the world. As recently as the 30th September 1942, Hitler repeated the lie in his speech at the Berlin Sports Palace. "I said," he reiterated, "that if Jewry started this war to overcome the Aryan people, it would not be the Aryans, but the Jews, who would be exterminated." In effect the lie suggests that the Jews are responsible for the War because they control international finance and that they design to dominate the world because they are international communists. This would imply, one would think, that Satan was attempting to cast out Satan, or Jews to cast out Jews. How, then, should their kingdom stand? Which, for all sensible people, reduces the proposition to absurdity. But as the Jews—it has been demonstrated again and again—neither control international finance nor direct the communist movement, the lie becomes even more fantastic, and therefore, presumably, according to Hitler, the more credible to the gullible.

It is particularly distressing that some of the unthinking are citizens of the Democracies, and that among the United Nations there are disciples of Hitler's mouthpiece, Dr. Goebbels, who glibly repeat his assertion that the Jews "aim at destroying the civilized nations of Europe and at founding a Jewish-international world regime that would subject all nations to their power."[1] One has to grant, of course, that the Nazi murderers are civilized, and that it is not they who are aiming at world domination.

---

1   Speaking at the Eighth Nazi Congress at Nuremberg, 1936.

"World Conquest!" exclaims Louis Golding bitterly. "And half the Jews of the world are menaced with disaster, and a third of them are on the brink of starvation, and there is not even enough solidarity of purpose among Jews to agree on the most elementary measures of self-defence! World Conquest! A sorry joke, my masters!"[1]

Now that the "Jewish Peril" has been applied by the Nazis to the intentions of Great Britain and the United States, the Christian citizens of these countries have the privilege of standing with the Jews in the same condemnation, and can decide for themselves how far the charge is justified. Ideologically, perforce, we are all Jews now; or as the late Pope Pius IX expressed it, "Spiritually we are Semites".[2]

Consideration of these circumstances ought to eliminate anti-semitism from America and the British Commonwealth. But will it? This evil is on the increase, and it still remains that far too little is known and far too much suspected to accomplish readily so desirable an end.

Something of the lie has stuck. Perhaps that is because it is not all lie. Perhaps there is somewhere an element of truth in it. There is!

I am not going to resurrect the forged *Protocols of the Elders of Zion,* which no Jews wrote and few Jews have

---

1 *The Jewish Problem* (Penguin Special), 1938.
2 He was addressing the directors of the Belgian Catholic Radio Agency in September 1936.

read. The terrible grain of truth is that the Jews are at the bottom of all this New Order business. They first inspired it, and they have never been able to stay out of it. They have a design for world domination, the domination of the world by the love of God and the principles of brotherhood, justice, and mutual service. If it had not been for Judaism the world would not have had these burning desires for a Messianic Age, for a Kingdom of God. Jews may foreswear Judaism, but they cannot shake off its obligations to strive for the Millennium, to promote by every means human betterment. Consciously, or unconsciously, they must work for a Brave New World. They are instinctive idealists. Their dreaming, their philosophy, their thirst for knowledge, their delving into the secrets of the Universe, their faith in human goodness, their pursuit of freedom and equality, their portrayal in music, drama, and the arts of the sorrows and hopes of mankind, all these are traceable to the heritage of Judaism.[1] One and all, in this way and that, they have

> "looked for a city which hath foundations, whose builder and maker is God."[2]

Or in the words of a modern non-Jewish poet:

> "That is the Jew of it, my Gentile friends,
> To see too far ahead and yet go on."[3]

---

1 See Appendix A.
2 *Epistle to the Hebrews,* ch. xi.
3 *John Brown's Body,* by Stephen Vincent Benet (Heinemann).

It all began with the Jewish Bible. Half a century ago Thomas Huxley wrote:

> "Throughout the history of the Western world the Scriptures have been the great instigators of revolt against the worst forms of clerical and political despotism. The Bible has been the Magna Charta of the poor and of the oppressed; down to modern times no State has had a constitution in which the interests of the people are so largely taken into account, in which the duties so much more than the privileges of rulers are insisted upon, as that drawn up for Israel in Deuteronomy and in Leviticus; nowhere is the fundamental truth that the welfare of the State, in the long run, depends on the uprightness of the citizen so strongly laid down.... The Bible is the most democratic book in the world."

What is the ultimate source of all the imaginings of a New World Order for the past two thousand years? It is the Bible. The Church of Rome, the Reformation, the Puritan Fifth Monarchists, the Age of Reason, the Nonconformist Religious Revival, Socialism and Communism, Democracy, all have been influenced directly or indirectly by the Bible.[1]

"Listen! the world is rising,

---

1   It is surely significant that, according to Dr. Wurm, Protestant Bishop of Wurtemberg, the Bible cannot now be published in Germany, though anti-Christian literature appears in mass editions (open letter to Dr. Goebbels in the Swedish paper *Trots Allt*).

> Seeking, unquiet, thrilling,
> Awakens the new century
> To new hopes and new visions.
> Men hear upon the mountains
> Strange and life-giving voices;
> Every soul seems to wait,
> And from that Book the signal
> For the new day shall come."[1]

Wherever men are marching towards the ultimate goal of the race, and under whatever banner, you will find Jews in the van of each contingent. They are driven on by a remorseless destiny—the Will of God itself set down in His Word.

This element in the creed of Judaism has been well expressed by Max L. Margolis. "I believe that Israel was chosen by God as His anointed servant to proclaim unto the families of mankind His truth; and, though despised and rejected by men, to continue as His witness until there come in through him the Kingdom of Peace and moral perfection, and the fulness of the knowledge of God, the true Community of the Children of the Living God."

The truth, then, behind the lie which Nazism and Fascism are at such pains to propagate is that the Jews believe in the Brotherhood of Man under the Fatherhood of

---

1   David Levi, Italian Jewish poet, 1846 (Trans. Mary A. Craig), quoted in A Book of Jewish Thoughts, p. 50 (Eyre & Spottiswoode).

God, that they are the enemies of the cult of racial superiority, lovers of peace and justice, opponents of aggression and tyranny. No wonder that there is no room for them in Hitler's 'New Order'.

But must we take the word of Jews for these claims? We should, but we need not. *The Book of Jewish Thoughts,* from which we have already quoted, and strongly recommend, contains a section devoted to "The Testimony of the Nations". We have space here for only two of a number of pregnant passages from the works of non-Jewish writers:

> "We Gentiles owe our life to Israel. It is Israel who has brought us the message that God is one, and that God is a just and righteous God, and demands righteousness of His children, and demands nothing else. It is Israel that has brought us the message that God is our Father. It is Israel who, in bringing us the divine law, has laid the foundations of liberty. It is Israel who had the first free institutions the world ever saw. It is Israel who has brought us our Bible, our prophets, our apostles. When sometimes our own unchristian prejudices flame out against the Jewish people, let us remember that all we have and all that we are we owe, under God, to what Judaism has given us."[1]

> "The religion of the Bible is well said to be revealed, because the great natural truth, that 'righteousness tendeth to life', is seized and exhibited there with such incomparable force and efficacy....

---

1   Lyman Abbott.

As long as the world lasts, all who want to make progress in righteousness will come to Israel for inspiration, as to the people who have had the sense for righteousness most glowing and strongest."[1]

Perish Judah! Then perish Humanity!

II

It was that great internationalist, Thomas Masaryk, first President of Czechoslovakia, who said: "He who looks up to Jesus as his M aster cannot be anti-semitic. You must be either one thing or the other, and if you are a Christian you cannot be an anti-semite."

The ultimate judgment of the anti-Jewish phobia of Nazism and Fascism rests on their repudiation of Christianity because of its "Jewishness The chant of the Hitler Youth must sound blasphemous in any decent ears:

> *"Wir wollen keine Christen sein,*
> *Denn Christus war ein Judenschwein."*

The refrain may be comprehended even by the reader who has no German, but may be rendered, however unpleasantly:

> "For Christianity we do not care a fig,
> Since Christ himself was but a Jewish pig."

---

1   Matthew Arnold.

According to Alfred Rosenberg the aim of the Nazi Party, self-confessed, is "to extirpate (from Germany) by all possible methods the Christian faith introduced in the year of disgrace 800". In a recent book, *Gott und Volk,* it is declared: "Every epoch has its sign. Two epochs and signs oppose each other to-day: the Cross and the Sword. The Sword is the weapon of the fighter, the sufferer drags the Cross.... We Germans have been called upon by fate to be the first to clash with Christianity."

So, then, the "Jewish Peril" is not only a Democratic Peril, but also a Christian Peril. Are we to hold that the International Christians have a secret conspiracy for world domination? One could surely quote liberally from Christian sources to prove that such is the aim of the Christian Faith. Is it not written in the *Revelation*: "The kingdoms of this world are become the kingdoms of our Lord, and of his Christ; and he shall reign for ever and ever"?[1]

If this be Christian Internationalism we can understand why Jewish Internationalism is considered dangerous. It is because, as the German Professor Gerhard Kittel has written, "at the cradle of modern Judaism stands the idea of humanity as superior to the concept of race" (*Die Judenfrage*).

For Jews and Christians there exists then a terrible and common peril to themselves. There is a common peril, and also a common purpose. In New Order building

---

1   Rev. xi. 14.

Judaism and Christianity go hand in hand: both are striving for the same noble ends.

In an article in *Harper's Magazine* the American writer, Stanley High, has these pertinent words:

> "The heaviest responsibility that the Jew has to bear is his gift to the world of the Old and New Testaments, the Prophets and Jesus. Encompassed in these gifts are the form and substance, the life and breath of the struggle for freedom which the powers of the world have most desperately sought to suppress. They hate the Jews not 'because they killed Christ' but *because they produced Him.* They know what short shifts can be made of their scheme of things if the succession of Jewish principles and the prophets in which Jesus stands takes hold and gets going."

Let there be an end, therefore, at least among Christians, of attention to the Nazi lie. Christian teaching and Christian efforts can only gain from an understanding of the kinship of Judaism. In the tremendous tasks that have to be accomplished in the coming years, the collaboration of both is needed. They have been brought together today as never before:[1] let us see to it that never again shall they find themselves in opposite camps.

---

1   See Appendix B.

Chapter II

What Is Judaism?

I

Because Judaism is understood to be the peculiar religion of a national community—the strictly private faith of the Jewish people—the average individual, not of Jewish birth, has seen no necessity to become acquainted with its tenets because they could not possibly apply to him: it would be committing almost an indecent trespass. Judaism could not be held to come into the category of universal religions, open to the acceptance of everyone. To become a believer in Judaism meant becoming a Jew, one of a clan rather than a church: one was bound to enter into a new physical and historical relationship with one's fellow-believers quite outside the ordinary experiences of a change of faith, to stop being a Gentile. This step would be so unusual, complicated, and 'queer', that one would not even think to look into the matter unless love for a Jewish man or maid lent to the strange relationship a sense of inevitability. The only alternative reason for investigating Judaism could be to gain a deeper insight into the meaning of Christianity or

Mohammedanism, of which this religion was the fore-runner.

Of course one knew that the Jews believed in One God, that they were bound by the Law of Moses, that they kept Saturday as the Sabbath, that they had Festivals—especially the Passover when they eat unleavened bread—that they had an annual 'Black' Fast, worshipped in synagogues where the men wore hats and were separated from the women and the language was Hebrew, that they had curious rites and customs mainly concerning Kosher food, that they regarded themselves as the Chosen People and looked for a Messiah who had not come yet. Such is the average idea of what Judaism means for Jews. To this may perhaps be added the conviction that Judaism was very narrow and exclusive, that it had a secret book called the Talmud, and that it was presided over by 'priests' called Rabbis.

The total inadequacy, let alone the partial inaccuracy, of this prevailing conception of Judaism would never give most people a moment's concern. It covers all that they are likely to want to know about Jews. It would be laughable if it were not so tragic, and the Jews themselves, who have been the principal actors in the tragedy, have seen the funny side of the ignorance about them.

There is the story of the schoolboy who, in reply to the question "What are Rabbis?" perpetrated the howler: "Rabbis are a disease, from which those who are bitten seldom recover." There is also the fact of the mediaeval

Christian controversialist who believed the Talmud was a person, and cited 'Rabbi Thalmud' as one of his authorities.

II

Judaism, like all great Faiths, has undergone a development: it has progressed with expanding knowledge of an expanding world; it has reached out to realms not contemplated by its earlier teachers. This is because it is essentially a religion of revelation, not a static but a dynamic revelation: it is a religion of movement. Those who think of Judaism as a spiritual attitude of cold formalism, narrow and insular, know almost nothing about it at all.

Judaism is founded on the Torah, commonly called the Law, and this misrendering of what is essentially a fluid body of teaching has been largely responsible for the false ideas of what Judaism really is. The Western world has as its background the Roman Law: it thinks in terms of binding enactments with decided penalties for infringement, and the conception of Justice as the administration of the Law as codified. This does not at all convey the implication of Torah, which regards Justice as mediatorial and interpretative, directing human relations according to divine principles which rest on an understanding sympathy and a penetration into the secrets of the heart. The famed case of the Judgment of Solomon in the matter of the two mothers[1] is typical of what the Torah stands for: it is feminine and intuitive.

Judaism therefore rejects the ferocity conveyed so well by Lewis Carroll in the termination of the mouse's 'tail' in *Alice in Wonderland*:

> "I'll try the whole cause,
>
> and condemn you to death."

Its Torah, to the contrary, is "a tree of life to them that lay hold upon it".[1] It is what people to-day call a "Way of Life".

> "Ye shall therefore keep My statutes and My judgments: which, if a man do, he shall live in them."[2]

As the Rabbis comment: "He shall live in them, not die in them." The Torah eternally keeps pace with the growth of Man's mind and the changes in his circumstances. It is never finished. This is why the Written Torah—in the Bible—must ever be supplemented by the Oral Torah, which translates its terms into contemporary action. It governs all relationships on the basis of the Unity and Fatherhood of God and the Brotherhood of Man.

There is the old Jewish story of the would-be proselyte to Judaism, who came to the meek and wise Rabbi Hillel (c. 30 B.C.), and insisted that he should be taught the whole

---

1   I *Kings* iii. 16-28.
1   *Prov.* iii. 18.
2   *Lev.* xviii. 5.

Torah while he stood on one leg. Said Hillel: "My son, what is hateful to thyself do not to thy fellow. That is the whole Torah: the rest is commentary."

Jesus, who lived and died in the Faith of Judaism, correctly summarized the religion of His people in the two fundamental commandments:

1. Hear, O Israel! The Lord our God is One Lord. And thou shalt love the Lord thy God with all thine heart, and with all thy soul, and with all thy might.

2. Thou shalt love thy neighbour as thyself.[1]

Everything in Judaism flows from this teaching. To accept these principles is to be a Jew in spirit, while remaining a non-Jew in other respects. The universalism of Judaism looks forward to the time when "The Lord shall be king over all the earth: in that day shall there be One Lord, and His name One."[2] To be a full Jew, however, requires a sense of mission, by reason of which other obligations and limitations are voluntarily assumed until this mission has been accomplished. I shall clearly explain this later.

---

1   *Mark* xii. 29-31 (*Deut.* vi. 4-5; *Lev*.xix. 18).
2   *Zech.* iv. 9.

III

"In the beginning God......" These opening words of the Hebrew Scriptures represent for all Jews the great reality, the fact behind all the phenomena of existence, the truth that gives meaning to being. God does not have to be proved because everything proclaims His abiding presence.

This faith in God is the subject of one of the most popular of all Jewish liturgical hymns composed about nine hundred years ago, and which I have translated as follows:

> "Lord of the Universe—Who reignedst
> ere aught that fashioned is was formed;
> Who in that very time was King proclaimed,
> when all things by His will were made;
> And after All shall ended be, shall still
> reign on, Alone, Tremendous.
> For He both Was, and Is,
> and Shall be ever in splendid state.
> And He is One. There is no other
> to compare with Him as fellow.
> Beginningless—Endless. To Him belong
> strength and dominion also.
> My God is He. Yea! my Redeemer liveth—
> Rock of my travail in time of stress.
> My Signal He, my Sure Retreat,

portion of my cup in the day that I call.

Sleeping and waking into His hand,

my spirit I commend,

And with my spirit my body also:

th' Eternal is with me—how should I fear!"

Who could fail to have complete trust in the Author of all Creation? How wonderful it is at any time when cares and anxieties beset us to be able to find peace in full dependence on the greater strength and wisdom of another, and how much more when that Other is the Absolute!

God is One and Indivisible. Judaism therefore rejects instinctively all teaching which would tend to weaken or detract from that consciousness of the All in the One, that would mar the perfection of concentration. The words of James, the brother of Jesus, are pure Jewish teaching, when he writes: "Every good gift and every perfect gift is from above, and cometh down from the Father of lights, with whom is no variableness, neither shadow of turning."[1] It is God Himself, without intermediary, Who is the Subject of Jewish worship, and the Eternal Spirit of his adoration. The Jew addresses God as "our Father, our King He stands in awe of the Divine, of that All-prevailing Majesty and Sovereignty. But at the same time he knows that he is a child of God, and enjoys the love of God. "Like as a father pitieth his children, so the Lord pitieth them that fear Him. For He knoweth our

---

1   *Jas.* i. 17. The New Testament document which the anti-semitic Luther impatiently described as a "straw epistle".

frame; He remembereth that we are dust."[1] The Divine
Father is ever accessible. "For thus saith the high and
lofty One that inhabiteth eternity, whose name is Holy; I
dwell in the high and holy place, with him also that is of
a contrite and humble spirit, to revive the spirit of the
humble, and to revive the heart of the contrite ones."[2]

Christians, who have very little acquaintance with Judaism, wrongly imagine that the Fatherhood of God was a
special revelation on the part of Jesus, and that before
this Jews did not have that close sense of communion
with the Almighty, that He was thought of as distant and
unapproachable.. This view is due in part, perhaps, to
the stress laid by Jews on God's holiness. But even here
it is the Jewish belief that all life should be invested with
this attribute of holiness: "Ye shall be holy: for I the Lord
your God am holy."[3] And ultimately, "shall there be upon
the bells of the horses 'holiness unto the Lord'... yea,
every pot in Jerusalem and in Judah shall be holiness
unto the Lord of hosts."[4] This is why ceremonial sancti-
fication enters so extensively into the practice of Judaism in daily life. Jews, indeed, have always cherished the
direct contact with the Supreme Being invited by the
concept of the Divine Fatherhood, and the very words
that Jesus taught His disciples to use in prayer—"Our
Father which art in Heaven"—were frequently on the lips
of Israel's sages.

----

1   *Psalm* ciii. 13-14.
2   *Isa.* lvii. 15.
3   Lev. xix. 2.
4   *Zech.* xiv. 20.21.

Those, on the other hand, who know Judaism well, have
been surprised and even dismayed by the extraordinary
familiarity with the Deity exercised by Jews, which
seemed to them to exhibit a lack of proper reverence.
This suggested that the idea of God's Fatherhood was being given an undue literalness. To be able to laugh and
joke in the Divine Presence was surely carrying things
too far. But that is the spirit of Judaism: it cannot con-
ceive of the Unsmiling God. Has He not Himself created
our capacity for joy and happiness, given us seasons of
festivity as well as solemnity? The synagogue has never
been invested with either the function or atmosphere of
a church: it is a communal home, and represents the ex-
tension of the individual family life to the larger family of
the Children of Israel. The Divine Presence is central in
this family scheme. That is why Judaism has often been
described as the religion of the home, and so much of its
practice is conducted there under the leadership of the
head of the household. As a consequence Jewish home
life has been held up as an example worthy of emulation,
and reflects the ideal which Jews have of the true relationship of all humanity. "Have we not all one Father?
Hath not one God created us? Why then do we deal
treacherously every man against his brother...?"[1] Cleric-
alism has no place in this scheme, where every man is a
minister of Divine things.

To expound the Jewish concept of God as that of a tribal
deity is a case of wishful thinking. He was and is for Jews
the "God of the spirit of all flesh."[2] This was the revela-

---

1   *Mal.* ii. 10.
2   *Nu.* xvi. 22

tion of Himself given to Israel. It is the basis of the universal ism of Judaism. Only those who wish deliberately to belittle the Jewish faith would permit themselves to express the view that Judaism has at any time subscribed to a narrower concept of the Almighty.

What then of the doctrine of the Chosen People? That, too, when rightly comprehended, is an evidence of Jewish universalism.

IV

The conviction that they were a superior race has been held by several peoples, and history records—without exception, I think—that they have been powerful, warlike peoples, boastful and arrogant. Such a conviction is wholly foreign to Judaism: the Jews themselves have never been powerful or particularly warlike. Their reactions to these 'superior race' manifestations has been stated often enough, and nowhere more clearly than in the Bible itself. Where some may see something grand and godlike the Hebrew prophet sees nothing but a predatory beast tearing with teeth and claws.[1] For him "the loftiness of man shall be bowed down, and the haughtiness of men shall be made low: and the Lord alone shall be exalted in that day."[2] No one who has studied the Bible could possibly fall into the error that there exists any kinship between the Jewish doctrine of the Chosen People and ideas of racial domination and superiority.

---

1   *Dan.* vii.
2   *Isa.* ii. 17.

And the fact that Jews are credited with having these ideas only shows how deeply rooted they are in the human mind, so that any other implication of an assertion of choice appears improbable and almost incomprehensible.

Yet both the nature and purpose of the choice find frequent and explicit mention in the Scriptures. Indeed, without this theme which runs right through its pages the Bible would lose much of its force and effect of unity. Written over many hundreds of years by men as varied in their character and station as the literature they produced is diverse in type and quality, there is this prevailing and urgent note of a people's calling and ordination to a divine world service—the mission of the People of the Book.

Judaism regards this mission as a fundamental reality: it invests the whole life of the Jew with a gravity of responsibility towards his fellows. It awakens in every springtide a passionate hope of accomplishment: it marks every autumn of unfulfilment with public contrition for failure and promise of amendment. The world's evil plight mirrors Israel's corporate sin.

Now this national obsession—if you will—with the idea that the salvation of the world depends on the Jewish people's righteousness and faithfulness to the Divine mandate is surely unique: it can have no possible kinship with theories of racial domination and superiority. It is in a suffering, sin-bearing capacity that the Jew sees his role. "In thee," God said to Abraham the Hebrew, "shall all families of the earth be blessed."[1] Here is the Bible's first intimation of something different from the common conception of the function of nationhood, something far removed from the lust for conquest and tribal egoism: it already marks out the path of service.

The seer Balaam, looking down from the heights upon the tents of Israel in the wilderness, was inspired to proclaim:

> "From the top of the rocks I see him,
>
> And from the hills I behold him:
>
> Lo, the people shall dwell alone,
>
> And shall not be reckoned among the nations."[2]

A people dwelling alone, not reckoned among the nations. Is it not for such a nation that the world has unwittingly been in quest, one which is separated from its problems of boundaries, and raw materials, and living-space, a nation that is international, intimately affected through its members by all the vicissitudes of states and yet so universal in outlook as to be capable of transcending the exclusiveness of more limited sovereignties?

To this people God declared through Moses: "Ye shall be unto Me a kingdom of priests, and an holy nation."[3] And again: "Ye shall be holy unto Me: for I the Lord am holy,

---

1 *Gen.* xi. 10.
2 *Nu.* xxiii. 9.
3 *Exod.* xix. 6.

and have severed you from other people, that ye should be Mine."[1]

The imagination of a holy nation is so august, so almost fantastic, that it seems impossible to credit human genius with it, especially in the barbaric age in which it was made known. This "choice" is undoubtedly of another order. The function of the Chosen People, as Judaism reveals it, is one of sacrificial and disinterested service without any self-commendation. The words of Jesus endorse this concept. "Ye know," he said, "that the princes of the Gentiles exercise dominion over them, and they that are great exercise authority upon them. But it shall not be so among you: but whosoever will be great among you, let him be your minister; and whosoever will be chief among you, let him be your servant."[2]

The choice certainly carries with it an offence which the nations must overcome before they can enter into blessing. This is the acid test of their worthiness to survive; for if they fail it is evident that justice and mercy are not in them. The life of every state is full of offences, offences against equity and morality, offences of squalor and poverty and disease, offences of craftiness and greed, of power-striving and pleasure-seeking. But the greatest offence of all is race-hatred, the hatred of another member of the human family. It is an incontestable fact of history that no anti-semitic nation has prospered; and it must be said with the most solemn emphasis that the eradication

---

1   *Lev.* xx. 26.
2   *Matt.* xx. 25-27.

of anti-semitism is an essential preliminary to lasting world peace. No other cause of friction between nations is as consequential as this ancient, deep-seated, and causeless enmity. The ordinance which has mysteriously distinguished one people from all the peoples which dwell on earth must be universally understood for what it truly implies in the operation of the Divine plan, as a vehicle for the redemption of nations.

So the would-be proselyte to Judaism must accept more than a religion: he must accept a national destiny of loneliness and humiliation, the life of the suffering servant of God, the mission and responsibility of world-healing.

In an older time, not so unlike the present, they used to ask such candidates: "'What makes thee desire to become a proselyte? Behold, seest thou not how the People is humbled and afflicted among the nations of the world, how many ills and sufferings come upon them,... how they are put to death,... and do not conduct their lives openly and freely like all the other peoples?' If he answer: 'I am not worthy to give my neck to the yoke of Him Who spake the word and the world came into existence,' they are to accept him immediately. If not, he is dismissed and goes on his way."[1]

---

1   *Gerim* 1.

V

The keyword of Judaism is "Remember". Only a very ancient people with a deep historic consciousness of Divine leading could found its conduct and its hopes on such a word.

"Pride and humiliation hand in hand
Walked with them through the world where'er they went;
Trampled and beaten were they as the sand,
And yet unshaken as the continent.

For in the background figures vague and vast Of patriarchs and prophets rose sublime,
And all the great traditions of the Past They saw reflected in the coming time.

And thus for ever with reverted look
The mystic volume of the world they read,
Spelling it backward, like a Hebrew book,
Till life became a Legend of the Dead."[1]

Again and again the Jew is bidden to remember, to rehearse the manifold mercies of God and to proclaim again His mighty acts. The corporate life of Israel has been spent in the presence of a hallowed chest, the Ark, in which reposed the eternal testimony; and still to-day in every synagogue a token Ark constitutes the essential

---

1 Longfellow, "Lines on the Jewish Cemetery at Newport".

property. Within each curtained closet the memorial scrolls are enshrined, richly garbed and crowned, repeatedly and reverently to be brought forth, unwrapped and read from in the hearing of the whole congregation. Remember! Ancient kings caused coffins to be borne through the banqueting chamber as a reminder of man's mortality; but the Ark of Israel is no *memento mori*: it is a symbol of life indestructible, the evidence of an Almighty Providence and Purpose.

But the past does not only guarantee the future: it sets the standard for present conduct. Of all memories that which most frequently recurs, is relived, and its lessons applied, is the memory of the centuries of slavery in Egypt: "Remember this day, in which ye came out from Egypt, out of the house of bondage."[1]

Man cherishes the boon of the seventh day rest from his labours. He owes it to the slavery of Israel. "Remember that thou wast a servant in the land of Egypt... therefore the Lord thy God commanded thee to keep the sabbath day."[2] The Jewish statute of limitations concerning the servitude and bankruptcy of a fellow-countryman arises from the same experience. "And if thy brother, an Hebrew man, or an Hebrew woman, be sold unto thee, and serve thee six years; then in the seventh year thou shalt let him go free. And when thou sendest him out free from thee, thou shalt not let him go away empty: thou shalt furnish him liberally out of thy flock, and out

---

1   *Exod.* xiii. 3.
2   *Deut.* v. 15.

of thy floor, and out of thy winepress: of that wherewith the Lord thy God hath blessed thee thou shalt give to him. And thou shalt remember that thou wast a bondman in the land of Egypt, and the Lord thy God redeemed thee."[1] So human dignity was safeguarded.

The right of all mankind to justice, the means of life, and the pursuit of happiness, is assured again on the basis of Israel's code which looks back to the Hebrew's unforgettable experience. "The Lord your God regardeth not persons, nor taketh reward: He doth execute the judgment of the fatherless and widow, and loveth the stranger, in giving him food and raiment. Love ye therefore the stranger: for ye were strangers in the Land of Egypt." [2] Equality, irrespective of race or creed, is a Jewish principle with the same origin. "The stranger that dwelleth with you shall be unto you as one born among yourselves, and thou shalt love him as thyself; for ye were strangers in the land of Egypt."[3] So was secured the welfare and title of foreign minorities to equality of treatment and opportunity.

All these things and many other wise and beneficent provisions are bound up for the Jew in that continual injunction to remember. Every day in the Jewish ritual the injunction is repeated and recalled by the individual as he recites the words of Scripture and exhibits on his person the phylacteries and fringed garment, and keeps a minute scroll nailed to the doors of his home. These

---

1   *Deut.* xv. 12-15.
2   *Deut.* x. 17-19
3   *Lev.* xix. 34.

noble precepts, he reads, "thou shalt teach diligently
unto thy children, and shalt talk of them when thou sit-
test in thine house, and when thou walkest by the way,
and when thou liest down, and when thou risest up. And
thou shalt bind them for a sign upon thine hand, and
they shall be for frontlets between thine eyes. And thou
shalt write them upon the door posts of thy house, and
upon thy gates."[1] And the fringed garment is "that ye
may look upon it, and remember all the commandments
of the Lord, and do them; and that ye go not about after
your own heart and your own eyes... that ye may remember... and be holy unto your God."[2] So Judaism inculcates in public and in private, at all times and seasons,
the love of God and Man, and sets ever before the Jew
the ideal of righteousness and responsibility; it charges
him with a mission of example, the end of which is to fulfil the highest hopes and aspirations of mankind. It envisages a world in which the law of lovingkindness
prevails, a world in which there are no aliens, where all
men are united in the Commonwealth of God.

---

1   *Deut.* vi. 6-9.
2   *Nu.* xv. 39-40.

Chapter III

The Vision of the Prophets

I

Over a great part of the world, consciously or unconsciously, the vision of the Jewish prophets is still the foundation and the inspiration prompting human effort to betterment.

As D.R. Davies has said: "The world owes an imperishable debt of gratitude to Old Testament prophecy. The prophets were the first philosophers of History. They saw in the events of time the operation of a God who was moral, not merely ontological and metaphysical.... In this attitude was the germ of universality, which came into consciousness in the Book of Jonah.... Prophecy redeemed History from casualness and meaninglessness. It informed it with Holy Spirit. It is, therefore, important that the prophetic vision should neither be obscured nor vulgarized. The Old Testament prophets are the most contemporary of all thinkers."[1]

---

1 *The Two Humanities,* p. 61.

By vulgarization, I take it that what Davies means is the equation of prophecy with prediction. This element in prophecy is a very minor factor, of prime significance mainly to the credulous and superstitious. The majestic sweep of the prophetic vision rolls unbroken over the lower peaks of incidental events to concentrate on the dateless altitudes of human crisis and achievement and distribute its stimulating and life-giving showers upon the whole fertile plain of history. The prophetic perception and proposition declares that because God IS, therefore there is Order, Purpose, and Progress in the affairs of Earth.

The prophets themselves frown on the quack astrologers and prognosticators, and the Jewish sages come down heavily on those given to calculating the time of the Messianic Age. This attitude is not due to lack of faith in the ultimate realization in history of the Divine plan, nor necessarily in later times to an apologetic obligation to escape from a dilemma of prophetic fulfilment, but rather to the negativing of those mischievous and misleading attempts of an illusory character to halt Man prematurely in his stride when only a fraction of his pilgrim journey is run and he has yet much to suffer and to learn. At such catastrophic moments in the march of events the cry must ever be repeated: "Speak unto the children of Israel, that they go forward."[1]

In this title to exercise the Divine mandate to urge on the people, and to set their faces steadfastly towards the high

---

1   *Exod.* xiv. 15.

destiny discerned shimmering in the golden haze of futurity, the prophets have their supreme function.

The language of the great prophets has thus become the solace and the incentive of generations. Seeing these visions men cannot help reaching out towards their realization: they must go forward, spiritually, socially, and politically.

II

In their reading of the riddle of creation the prophets pay particular regard to the implications of Monotheism and the calling out of a Holy Nation. If the families of the earth were ever to be reunited it could only be through a replacement of belief in national and local divinities by faith in the One supreme God and Father. Gods many and lords many, national and party emblems, could only perpetuate spiritual divisions and prejudices between people. Only a universal acknowledgment of the Unity of God could bring about the unity and brotherhood of Man. Monotheism, therefore, was a vital social and political creed, and the Holy Nation was required to proclaim it. "Ye are My witnesses, saith the Lord, that I am God."[1]

The world of to-day offers a striking illustration of the results of human failure to recognize the fundamental principle of the Divine Unity. States are rent by warring factions with their rival colours and insignia. The Powers

---

1 *Isa.* xliii. 12.

strive with each other to the death under the banners of
their respective ideologies. The tribal gods, partially ban-
ished, have reappeared under new names, but still with
the same evil characteristics, still lustful, still demanding
holocausts and the casting of infants into the flames.

Yet out of the chaos is to come order, the true New Order, and the Jew is to be the symbol and the mediator of
it. "Thus saith the Lord of hosts, It shall yet come to pass,
that there shall come people, and the inhabitants of
many cities: and the inhabitants of one city shall go to
another, saying, Let us go speedily to pray before the
Lord, and to seek the Lord of hosts; I will go also. Yea,
many people and strong nations shall come to seek the
Lord of hosts in Jerusalem, and to pray before the Lord.
Thus saith the Lord of hosts, In those days it shall come
to pass, that ten men shall take hold out of all languages
of the nations, even shall take hold of the robe of him
that is a Jew, saying, We will go with you: for we have
heard that God is with you."[1]

Through God's Servant-Nation His dominion is to be established on earth. "The kingdom and dominion, and the
greatest of the kingdom under the whole heaven, shall be
given to the people of the saints of the Most High, whose
kingdom is an everlasting kingdom, and all dominions
shall serve and obey Him."[2] It is to be a real world government, as we are only now beginning more exactly to
picture and work for it, and not a kingdom in the clouds.

---

1   *Zech.* vii. 20-23.
2   *Dan.* vii. 27.

Contrary to a common belief the Bible nowhere promises a celestial future for humanity. "The heavens, even the heavens are the Lord's; but the earth hath He given unto the children of men."[1] Those who have suffered pain and hardship here may pray for a blessed release into an existence free from care and sorrow: they may sing with longing of mansions in the skies, just as the despised negro feelingly chants "Go down Moses: set my people free." Yet surely the consoling doctrine is an indictment of the world as man in his neglect of God has made it. The Jews have been piously reproved for their earthly hopes; but they have been entirely in the right; for God has promised to make His dwelling among men. The doctrine of the saints living with the angels has invited a justifiable accusation of otherworldliness, implying a lack of proper concern for the pressing problems of mankind. The seer is better informed of the truth of God when he envisages not only a new heaven, but also a new earth in which righteousness dwells.

And so the prophets look forward to redeemed Man, living in a redeemed earth under God the Redeemer of All.

"In the last days it shall come to pass, that the mountain of the house of the Lord shall be established in the top of the mountains, and it shall be exalted above the hills; and all people shall flow unto it. And many, nations shall come, and say, Come, and let us go up to the mountain of the Lord, and to the house of the God of Jacob; and He will teach us of His ways, and we will walk in His paths: for the law shall go forth of Zion, and the word of the

---

1   *Ps.* cxv. 16.

Lord from Jerusalem. And He shall judge among many people, and rebuke strong nations afar off; and they shall beat their swords into plowshares, and their spears into pruning-hooks: nation shall not lift up a sword against nation, neither shall they learn war any more. But they shall sit every man under his vine and under his fig tree and none shall make them afraid: for the mouth of the Lord of hosts hath spoken it."[1]

This noble anticipation of a world at peace carries with it, as we must never forget, the means by which such peace can be realized—it is through willing obedience to the revealed laws of God. The cessation of war on any other basis is impossible.

This is what Judaism teaches, and it is the reason why—as one of its exponents has well said—"the Jew who is true to himself will labour with especial energy in the cause of peace. His religion, his history, his mission, all pledge him to a policy of peace, as a citizen as well as an individual. The war-loving Jew is a contradiction in terms. The 'Man of Sorrows' must beware of helping, however remotely, to heap sorrow upon others."[2]

III

But did not the prophets speak of a Messiah, who would usher in the age of peace? Yes, they did; and the belief is bound up with the coming of the New World Order as

---

1   *Mic.* iv. 1-4.
2   Morris Joseph, *Judaism as Creed and Life.*

Judaism understands it. Here is that point at which Jews and Christians have hitherto diverged and gone their separate ways; for to Christians the Messiah has come and to Jews he is not come yet.

Let us try and grasp the Jewish position. It is essentially this, that the Messiah, the Messianic People, and the Messianic Age are three inseparables. All must be together when the day of redemption dawns. Until the Spirit of God is manifested in the conduct of nations, the time of Israel's trials will not yet be over. Until the sufferings of Israel are ended, the Messianic Age cannot come. Until the Messianic Age comes, the Messiah will not be revealed. So Judaism, through bitter experience, watches the world, watches the state of the Jews, and watches every Messianic claimant. Only when *all* the signs are present will the day of deliverance have arrived.

For its watching brief Judaism has its great test passage in the prophetic writings, which it has already applied on memorable historical occasions when it seemed that the longed-for time might indeed be at hand.

"And there shall come forth a rod out of the stem of Jesse, and a branch shall grow out of his roots. And the spirit of the Lord shall rest upon him, the spirit of wisdom and understanding, the spirit of counsel and might, the spirit of knowledge and fear of the Lord; and shall make him of quick understanding in the fear of the Lord: and he shall not judge after the sight of his eyes, neither reprove after the hearing of his ears: but with righteousness shall he judge the poor, and reprove with equity for the meek of the earth: and he shall smite the earth with the rod of his mouth, and with the breath of his lips shall he slay the wicked. And righteousness shall be the girdle of his loins, and faithfulness the girdle of his reins. The wolf also shall dwell with the lamb, and the leopard shall lie down with the kid; and the calf and the young lion and the fatling together; and a little child shall lead them. And the cow and the bear shall feed; their young ones shall lie down together: and the lion shall eat straw like the ox. And the sucking child shall play on the hole of the asp, and the weaned child shall put his hand on the cockatrice' den. They shall not hurt nor destroy in all my holy mountain: for the earth shall be full of the knowledge of the Lord, as the waters cover the sea.

"And in that day there shall be a root of Jesse, which shall stand for an ensign of the people; to it shall the Gentiles seek: and his rest shall be glorious. And it shall come to pass in that day, that the Lord shall set his hand again the second time to recover the remnant of his people, which shall be left, from Assyria, and from Egypt, and from Pathros, and from Cush, and from Elam, and from Shinar, and from Hamath, and from the islands of the sea. And he shall set up an ensign for the nations, and shall assemble the outcasts of Israel, and gather together the dispersed of Judah from the four corners of the earth."[1]

---

1   *Isa.* xi. i—12.

So for the prophet, as for Judaism ever since, the three signs must be simultaneously evident, the sign of the Son of David, the sign of Israel's Ingathering, and the sign of a Peaceable Godfearing Humanity. Together they constitute that

> *... far-off divine event*
> *To which the whole creation moves.*

Chapter IV

The Message of Judaism to The Ancient World

I

The Jewish dispersion among the nations began centuries before the Fall of Jerusalem in A.D. 70. In Mesopotamia and Persia, Egypt and North Africa, Asia Minor, Greece and Rome, and even further west, Jews settled increasingly after the Babylonian Exile. Great cities had their Jewish Quarter. Egypt had a Jewish Temple rivalling that of Jerusalem. In many places Jews rose to high civic office. Statutes and ordinances safeguarded their freedom of life and worship. Their Scriptures and other works were rendered into Greek.

The effect of the Diaspora was for the first time to bring the world at large into close contact with Jewish thought and faith. Poets and philosophers of the nations found much at which to mock and scoff in Jewish customs and beliefs, from the vindictive Apion to the satirical Juvenal, who wrote:

"Some men who had a sabbath-fearing father,
Worship no god except the clouds and sky,
And deem swine's flesh as sacred as a man's,
Because their father did; then clip their foreskins,
And holding in contempt the Roman laws,
They learn and keep and fear the Jewish code,
Whate'er says Moses in his mystic volume...
Their father is to blame, who passed in sloth
The seventh day and therein would do no work."[1]

But on the whole there can be no doubt that the concept of One Universal God, invisible and indivisible, and the austere morality of the Jewish tenets created a deep and widespread impression and exercised a profound influence for good, and many were the Gentiles attending regularly at Jewish worship and even adopting Judaism completely or in part.

On the other hand Judaism itself, by this enlargement of its horizon, and the daily association of Jews with non-Jews, was forced to consider more adequately world problems and world behaviour, and to find its defenders and apologists for its own ideals and way of life.

One product of this adventuring beyond the established spiritual boundaries was Hellenistic Judaism, which sought to meet the Gentile philosophers on their own ground. Its chief exponent was Philo Judaeus, a contemporary of Jesus, who carried the heritage of Judaism into

---

1   Juv. *Satire*, xiv. 97.

the camp of the Stoics and Eclectics, and showed Moses as the type of perfect man.

Another product was Christianity, which set forth the Messianic Hope in Cosmic terms, and announced a Salvation by Grace open to all men irrespective of race if they would abandon idolatry and serve the One True God and give allegiance to His anointed son. Its principal protagonist was the Apostle Paul, who revealed Jesus Christ as the divinely appointed world redeemer.

A third product was Apocalyptic Judaism, which employed cryptic imagery, visions, and mysteries, in order to convey a sense of the Divine plan for humanity and the certainty of His impending judgment on the sinful. Most of the apocalyptic literature is pseudonymous, so that one cannot speak of any particular individual, but one of the means chosen to circulate the warnings of Judaism to an evil age was a system of deft interpolations in the writings of Gentile authors of repute.

In most of this religious propaganda the emphasis is on the doctrine of the existence of the One God, a Day of Judgment for the world, and the future felicity of the Righteous.

But orthodox Judaism was also touched in the same period with the universalist spirit. This is seen in the practice of offering daily in the Temple sacrifices on behalf of all the nations, and the recitation by the Jewish people of that flower of the Hebrew Liturgy, the '*Alenu* prayer, part of which reads:

> "Therefore do we wait for Thee, O Lord our God, soon to behold Thy mighty glory, when Thou wilt remove the abominations from the earth, and idols shall be exterminated; when the world shall be regenerated by the kingdom of the Almighty, and all the children of flesh invoke Thy name; when all the wicked of the earth shall be turned unto Thee. Then shall all the inhabitants of the world perceive and confess that unto Thee every knee must bend, and every tongue be sworn. Before Thee, O Lord our God, shall they kneel and fall down, and unto Thy glorious name give honor. So will they accept the yoke of Thy kingdom, and Thou shalt be King over them speedily forever and aye. For Thine is the kingdom, and to all eternity Thou wilt reign in glory, as it is written in Thy Torah: 'The Lord shall reign forever and aye.' And it is also said: And the Lord shall be King over all the earth; on that day the Lord shall be One and His name be One.'"[1]

II

In the domain of Apologetic the work of Flavius Josephus against the anti-semitic slanders of Apion is particularly noteworthy. Like other writers he also lays stress on the Jewish mission to the nations, which by a Divine ordinance has set Israel apart for hierarchic service.

---

1   *Jewish Encyclopaedia*, vol. i. p. 337.

"What form of government then can be more holy than this?" he asks. "What more worthy kind of worship can be paid to God than we pay, where the entire body of the people are prepared for religion, where an extraordinary degree of care is required in the priests, and where the whole polity is so ordered as if it were a certain religious solemnity? For what things foreigners, when they solemnize such festivals, are not able to observe for a few days' time, and call them Mysteries and Sacred Ceremonies, we observe with great pleasure and an unshaken resolution during our whole lives." He goes on to speak of God as the Absolute and the Invisible, revealed in His Creation, and adds, "All men ought to follow this Being, and to worship Him in the exercise of virtue; for this way of worship of God is the most holy of all others. There ought also to be but one temple for One God; for likeness is the constant foundation of agreement. This temple ought to be common to all men, because He is the common God of all men.... And for our duty at the sacrifices themselves, we ought in the first place to pray for the common welfare of all, and after that our own; for we are made for fellowship one with another; and he who prefers the common good before what is peculiar to himself is above all acceptable to God."[1]

Those who talk easily of Jewish insularity in the first century of the Christian Era may be surprised at such

---

1 *Against Apion*, bk. ii. § 23-24.

sentiments, which exhibit an exalted Universalism and Spiritual Socialism.

Then what of so-called Legalistic Judaism, so frequently described as narrow and burdensome? Let us quote Josephus again:

> "We have already demonstrated that our laws have been such as have always inspired admiration and imitation into all other men: nay, the earliest Grecian philosophers, though in appearance they observed the laws of their own countries, yet did they, in their actions and philosophic doctrines, follow our legislator, and instructed men to live sparingly, and to have friendly communication one with another. Nay, further, the multitude of mankind itself have had a great inclination for a long time to follow our religious observances; for there is not any city of the Grecians, nor any of the barbarians, nor any nation whatsoever, whither our custom of resting on the seventh day hath not come, and by which our fasts and lighting up lamps, and many of our prohibitions as to our food, are not observed; they also endeavour to imitate our mutual concord with one another, and the charitable distribution of our goods, and our diligence in our trades, and our fortitude in undergoing the distresses we are in, on account of our laws; and what is here matter of the greatest admiration, our law hath no bait of pleasure to allure men to it, but it prevails by its own force; and as God Himself pervades all the

world, so hath our law passed through all the world also....

"As to the laws themselves, more words are unnecessary, for they are visible in their own nature, and appear to teach not impiety, but the truest piety in the world. They do not make men hate one another, but encourage people to communicate what they have to one another freely; they are enemies to injustice, they take care of righteousness, they banish idleness and expensive living, and instruct men to be content with what they have, and to be laborious in their callings; they forbid men to make war from a desire of getting more, but make men courageous in defending the laws; they are inexorable in punishing malefactors; they admit no sophistry of words, but are always established by actions themselves, which actions we ever propose as surer demonstrations than what is contained in writing only; on which account I am so bold as to say that we are become the teachers of other men, in the greatest number of things, and those of the most excellent nature only; for what is more excellent than inviolable piety? What is more just than submission to laws, and what is more advantageous than mutual love and concord?"[1]

III

With the lofty teachings of Pauline Christianity, which I must regard as an expression of Judaism, the non-Jew-

---

1   *Against Apion*, bk. ii. § 40-42.

ish reader will be so familiar that quotation is needless. I pass on, therefore, to Visionary Judaism outside the Bible. The poets and philosophers of the ancient Gentile world have written indeed of the Golden Age and the Ideal State. Virgil and Plato are not lonely names in this connection; but the seers of Judaism are all at one in their passionate faith in the redemption of human society: for them there could be no other culmination to the story of mankind. The ways of God to men must be justified. Where others might be hopeless they had an assured hope. Where others might doubt they had certainty.

Here then in three representative extracts speaks Jewish utopianism of some two thousand years ago.

The first quotation I take from the *Book of Enoch*.

> "And in those days will the whole earth be tilled in righteousness and will all be planted with trees and be full of blessing. And all desirable trees will be planted on it, and vines will be planted on it; the vine which is planted thereon will yield wine in abundance, and of all the seed which is sown thereon will each measure bear ten thousand, and each measure of olives will yield ten presses of oil. And cleanse Thou the earth from all oppression, and from all unrighteousness, and from all sin, and from all godlessness, and from all uncleanness which is wrought upon the earth: destroy them from off the earth. And all the children of men shall become righteous, and all nations shall offer

Me adoration and praise, and all will worship Me. And the earth will be cleansed from all corruption, and from all sin, and from all punishment and torment, and I will never again send them upon it, from generation to generation. And in those days I will open the store chambers of blessing which are in the heaven, so as to send them down upon the earth over the work and labour of the children of men. Peace and justice will be wedded throughout all the days of the world and throughout all the generations of the world."[1]

The second passage is from the *Apocalypse of Baruch*:

"And it will come to pass, when He has brought low everything that is in the world, and has sat down in peace for the age on the throne of His kingdom, that joy will then be revealed, and rest appear. And then healing will descend in dew, and disease will withdraw, and anxiety and anguish and lamentation will pass from amongst men, and gladness will proceed through the whole earth. And no one shall again die untimely, nor shall any adversity suddenly befall. And judgments, and revilings, and contentions, and revenges, and blood, and passions, and envy, and hatred, and whatsoever things are like these shall go into condemnation when they are removed. For it is these very things which have filled this world with evils, and on account of these the life of man has been greatly troubled. And wild beasts will come from

---

1   *Enoch*, chs. x. -xi.

the forest and minister unto men, and asps and dragons will come forth from their holes to submit themselves to a little child. And women will no longer then have pain when they bear, nor will they suffer torment when they yield the fruit of the womb. And it shall come to pass in those days that the reapers will not grow weary, nor those that build be toilworn; for the works will of themselves speedily advance with those who do them in much tranquillity. For that time is the consummation of that which is corruptible, and the beginning of that which is not corruptible. Therefore those things which were predicted will belong to it: therefore it is far away from evils, and near to those things which die not. This is the bright lightning which came after the last dark waters."[1]

Finally a Jewish extract from the *Sibylline Oracles*:

"But when this destined day is fully come, a great rule and judgment shall come upon men. For the fertile earth shall yield her best fruit of corn and wine and oil; it shall gush out in sweet fountains of white milk: the cities shall be full of good things, and the fields with fatness; no sword shall come against the land, not shout of war; nor shall the earth again be shaken, deeply groaning: no war nor drought shall afflict the land, no dearth nor hail to spoil the crops, but deep peace over all the earth; king shall live as friend to king to the bound of the age, and the Immortal shall establish in the starry

---

1   *Baruch*, chs. lxxiii-lxxiv.

heaven one law for men over all the face of the earth for all the doings of hapless mortals."[1]

In such glowing colours did Judaism express its invincible conviction that one day the eternal promise would be fulfilled in a true New World Order. Its poets sang the Hallelujah song whose triumphant notes have rung down the centuries, inspiring human effort and endeavour, proclaiming the era of peace and goodwill even in the darkest night of failure and despair.

In their better-known Jewish-Christian form, in the *Book of Revelation*, or *Apocalypse of John*, these sentiments have been the consolation of millions in life and death:

> "And I heard as it were the voice of a great multitude, and as the voice of many waters, and as the voice of mighty thunderings, saying, Alleluia: for the Lord God omnipotent reigneth....
>
> "And I heard a great voice out of heaven, saying, Behold, the tabernacle of God is with men, and He will dwell with them, and they shall be His people, and God Himself shall be with them, and be their God. And God shall wipe away all tears from their eyes; and there shall be no more death, neither sorrow, nor crying, neither shall there be any more pain: for the former things are passed away."[2]

---

1   *Sibylline Oracles*, bk. iii., § 742-760.
2   *Rev.* xix. 6; xxi. 3-4.

So Zion, of old, brought glad tidings to a stricken world, thrilling it and challenging it with the message of right-eousness and the fruits thereof, universal in application, laying upon the soul of man the ineffaceable imprint of the finger of God.

INTERVAL

The Great Test

"The heroism of the defenders of every other creed fades into insignificance before this martyr people, who for thirteen centuries confronted all the evils that the fiercest fanaticism could devise, enduring obloquy and spoliation and the violation of the dearest ties, and the infliction of the most hideous sufferings, rather than abandon their faith.

"Persecution came to the Jewish nation in its most horrible forms, yet surrounded by every circumstance of petty annoyance that could destroy its grandeur, and it continued for centuries their abiding portion. But above all this the genius of that wonderful people rose supreme. While those around them were grovelling in the darkness of besotted ignorance; while juggling miracles and lying relics were the themes on which almost all Europe was expatiating; while the intellect of Christendom, enthralled by countless superstitions, had sunk into a deadly torpor, in which all love of inquiry and search for truth were abandoned, the Jews were still pursuing the path of knowledge, amassing learning, and stimulating progress with the same unflinching constancy that they manifested in their faith."—W.E.H. Lecky, 1865.

INTERVAL

The Great Test

I

What for Judaism was its great period, roughly from the second to the fifteenth century, this little book must pass over almost in silence. The reason is tragic, but clear. For the larger part of this time the Jew was an outcast, the chattel of Church and Ruler. He was denied all the ordinary rights of humanity, insecure in his dwelling, uncertain of his life, the prey of bigotry and mob violence, debarred from most occupations, liable to summary expulsion from every city and land where he might find a temporary home, a wanderer on the face of God's fair earth.

In all history no other people has been subjected to such a fiery test of its faith in God and Man. If individuals are tempted through the experience of evil and suffering to deny the existence of a just God, much more the Jew! If the downtrodden and oppressed may be driven to despair of human brotherhood, much more the Jew! Yet from this stern ordeal the Jew emerged triumphant: his faith had saved him.

Has any other religion proved its power like Judaism to enable its adherents to accept with patience the worst things that can befall, not only at some exalted moment of martyrdom, but on and on from generation to genera-

tion, and century to century, through a seemingly end-
less night? And not only to accept with patience, but to
exhibit as a consequence a singular lack of hatred and
vindictiveness towards the authors of such sufferings, to
bless rather than to curse, to preserve dignity and virtue,
and above all to believe utterly in the love and justice of
God and the ultimate regeneration of all mankind?
When one reads the story of the Jews one must be con-
vinced of the truth of God and of a coming World Order,
for one has seen the Sermon on the Mount practised in
the very Valley of the Shadow of Death.

> "Be thou the cursed," said the Rabbis, "not he who
> curses. Be of them that are persecuted, not of them
> that persecute. Look at Scripture: there is not a
> single bird more persecuted than the dove; yet God
> has chosen her to be offered up on His altar. The
> bull is hunted by the lion, the sheep by the wolf,
> the goat by the tiger. And God said, 'Bring Me a
> sacrifice, not from them that persecute, but from
> them that are persecuted.'"

II

It might be considered that living under such conditions
and restrictions, limited, cramped, and proscribed, the
Jew might hold that he was thereby absolved from his
mission, that he could remain passive until better times,
seeing that the world had done its utmost to make it impossible for him to render any useful service to his fel-

lows. None could have blamed him for standing sullen and aloof, washing his hands of all responsibility.[1]

But this was not the Jewish view; and whenever opportunity offered, Jews were found labouring for the advancement of knowledge and the welfare of humanity.

"The Jews could be driven into their Ghettos, but it was not so easy to drive them into a Ghetto life. To the horror of pious Christians, they persisted in retaining outside interests, and in collaborating effectively (so far as it was humanly possible) in the activities of the outside world.... When the Dark Ages lost all idea of the magnificent heritage of Greece—its philosophy and its medicine and its science—it was the Jews, together with the Arabs, who treasured it and yet further developed it.... It was thus largely through the devious medium of translations from Greek to Arabic, and from Arabic to Hebrew, and from Hebrew to Latin, that the first breath of the Renaissance stirred Europe; and without these Jewish intermediaries the background even of Dante would be unrecognizable....

"Such activities did not preclude original work:

---

1 Christian students of prophecy regard this interval of the *Goluth* (Exile), aptly enough, as "The Times of the Gentiles" spoken of in the New Testament (*Luke* xxi. 24). But they also talk of "The Jewish clock standing still," which is true only in the sense of an imposed limitation of opportunity.

on the contrary, they incited to it. Notwithstanding
the prohibition which obtained in the Christian
world, the names of thousands of Jewish physi-
cians of the Middle Ages have been preserved, in-
cluding men like Isaac Israeli, who were among the
fathers of mediæval medicine. The medical works
of the great Maimonides were studied at the uni-
versities of Christian Europe down to the eight-
eenth century.... On the threshold of modern
times, great names emerge like those of Garcia
d'Orta, the founder of tropical medicine, and
Rodrigo de Castro, the founder of gynaecology.
Maimonides is, of course, best remembered as a
philosopher, and to his speculations St. Thomas
Aquinas was indebted for a good deal in that great
system of thought which mediaeval Europe regarded as fundamental.

"Other Ghetto scholars turned to astronomy, and
were responsible for many noteworthy innova-
tions. The greatest centre of map-making in the
fourteenth century was the Jewish quarter of
Palma, in Majorca, where the discoveries of Marco
Polo were first recognized and incorporated in rep-
resentations of the contemporary world.... The
famous nautical school at Sagres, the cradle of the
Portuguese discoveries which resulted in the
rounding of the Cape and the opening of the sea
route to India, was first directed by a Majorcan
Jew... and both the improved astrolabe, and the
Jacob's Staff—the two indispensable instruments

for nautical observation used by all the explorers of the period—were invented by Jewish Rabbis."[1]

These accomplishments, which might be greatly multiplied, are instanced to show the progressive spirit which Judaism inspired. Just as in his physical existence the Jew was forced always to "move on, move on," so in his mental and spiritual life there could be no standing still. The pillar of cloud went in front by day, the pillar of fire by night, as he journeyed ever onward from slavery to freedom, from the House of Bondage to the Promised Land, still drawing after him a mixed multitude—sometimes they knew not how or why—into the experience of a new fellowship, the fellowship of the Sons of God.

---

1 Louis Golding, *The Jewish Problem* (Penguin Special), pp. 71-73.

PART TWO

Evangel for Nations

"In a free state, it is not the Christian that rules the Jew. neither is it the Jew that rules the Christian; it is Justice that rules."—Leopold Zunz, 1859.

"On the High Festivals the Jew thinks not only of himself, but of peace and blessedness for all mankind. In the most ancient and solemn part of the services, both of the New Year and of the Day of Atonement, he prays God to hasten the time when the mighty shall be just and the just mighty; when all the children of men shall form one band of brotherhood; when national arrogance and oppression shall have passed away, like so much smoke from the earth."—J. H. Hertz, Chief Rabbi, 1924.

Chapter I

Anonymous Ben Anonymous

I

In representing the impact of Judaism on Ancient and Mediaeval Society I have indicated that its influence was mainly indirect and conveyed indirectly by pseudonymous propaganda, parable, and allegory. To a very appreciable extent this oblique method was imposed on the Jew by his lack of security, his uneasy position in the midst of a hostile world. Judaism could not lead men towards betterment: it could only by its revelation of Truth inspire and prompt them to take the initiative, with, or more often without, acknowledgment. It is this fact that has created the impression of Judaism as a "hidden hand", as a power "behind the scenes". The most loosely knit and incoherent community in the world has thus acquired a reputation for secret purposefulness and mysteriously organized activity which has no real existence in the form of any Judaic cabal, conclave, or confederacy. But there is, of course, no getting away from the evidence that Judaism is a leavening activating force, which in devious ways has been working through the ages for the overthrow of injustice and oppression: it is the mystery of the Kingdom of God, which Jesus set forth in his parables.[1]

So Judaism stood behind Christianity in its struggle with Roman Imperialism, behind the Renaissance and the Reformation in the fight against Superstition and Intolerance, behind Rationalism in the war for Human Liberty, behind Communism in the demand for Social Justice, behind Democracy in its present opposition to Totalitarian Aggression. It has stood and will ever stand behind the manifestations of spiritual aspiration, enlightenment, and progress. The enemies of these things will always label this influence as malign, sinister, and destructive, and their friends will all too frequently fail to give credit where it is due. But this does not really matter. What does matter is that the will of God should be done on earth.

There is a rabbinical maxim that "He that incites another to the performance of a good deed is greater than he that does the deed." And the principles of Judaism as enshrined in its Sacred Literature are in this sense greater than the resultant achievements of individuals and movements. But when I have said that Judaism has stood behind the light-bringing and civilizing activities of the West I do not mean to suggest that it has been in every case consciously directive, or that Jews have necessarily played a leading part. What I do claim is that it has

---

1   E.g., in the parables of the Leaven, the Grain of Mustard Seed, the Hidden Treasure, the Pearl of Great Price, etc., *Matt,* xiii., *Lk.* xiii.

been none the less the effective cause, whether realized or not. It has usually been the anti-God and anti-social forces that have been most acutely aware of the true source of their discomfiture.

Fortunately, this has not been so invariably, as illustrated by the following testimonies.

> "The moral feelings of men have been deepened and strengthened, and also softened, and almost created by the Jewish prophets. In modern times we hardly like to acknowledge the full force of their words, lest they should prove subversive to society."[1]

> "That there is one day in the week that the working man may call his own, one day in the week on which the hammer is silent and the loom stands idle, is due, through Christianity, to Judaism—to the code promulgated in the Sinaitic wilderness. And who that considers the waste of productive forces can doubt that modern society would be not merely happier, but richer, had we received as well as the Sabbath day the grand idea of the Sabbath year, or, adapting its spirit to our changed conditions, secured in another way an equivalent reduction of working hours."[2]

"The ancient psalm still keeps its music, and this is but the outer sign of its spiritual power, which remains as near and intimate to our needs, human and divine, as in

---

1   Benjamin Jowett.
2   Henry George.

David's day. So, indeed, it seems to have remained through all the centuries—the one body of poetry which has gone on, apart from the change of races and languages, speaking with a voice of power to the heart of men."[1]

> "The greater the intellectual progress of the ages, the more fully will it be possible to employ the Bible not only as the foundation, but as the instrument, of education."[2]

> "I believe that Jewish wisdom is more all-human and universal than any other, and this not only because of its immemorial age, not only because it is the firstborn, but also because of the powerful humaneness that saturates it, because of its high estimate of man."[3] "No greater moral change ever passed over a nation than passed over England during the years of the reign of Elizabeth, England became the people of a book, and that book was the Bible.... The effect of the Bible in this way was simply amazing. The whole temper of the nation was changed. A new conception of life and of man superseded the old. A new moral and religious impulse spread through every class."[4]

To the same effect one might cite many more authorities.[5] The spiritual and moral conflict which the Jewish contribution has emphasized must be resolved by every

---

1   Ernest Rhys.
2   Goethe.
3   Maxim Gorky.
4   J. R. Green.
5   See "The Testimony of the Nations," *Book of Jewish Thoughts.*

man for himself. He can decide either that "The Jews are our misfortune" or that "Salvation is of the Jews".

It remains that the Jew can with difficulty say anything directly; he is almost bound until the New World comes to continue anonymous: he must serve incognito. None the less he must serve God and Man, though in many garbs and guises, and sometimes through substitutes.[1] He saves others: himself he cannot save. The powers that have dominion over this present world have dictated his role: they insist that the servant of all should be made to appear as a malefactor.

II

Many people have asked why Judaism does not come into the open, why it does not trumpet forth its challenge to evil, and proclaim its gospel up and down the earth. I have given part of the answer to this question: that anti-Jewish feeling prevents it, that the message would not be accepted from Jews as Jews. The Jew can only say, "Blessed is he, whosoever shall not be offended in me." But it would be wrong to suggest that this is the whole answer. Another part of it is to be found in the nature of the Jewish mission, which imposes a certain separateness on the People of God until its task be ended in the Messianic Age. Judaism can extend no general invitation to share its limitations and responsibilities, for its adherents are to be a kingdom of priests, and not all are called to the priesthood. It would be like asking the Christian

---

1   See Appendix A.

clergy to require everyone to enter holy orders. To some
extent the Papacy is in the position of Judaism, in that
its function is to affirm moral and spiritual principles
rather than to enter directly into controversy and political action.[1]

I do not desire to conceal the setting in of spiritual de-
generation, which where operative leaves the Jew with
nothing but a self-esteeming clannishness, and no less
makes a sanctimonious clique of a body of Christian
clergy. Such a vaunting of Jew over Gentile, or clergy
over laity, brings both into evil repute, and very justly. It
is a danger that can only be avoided by true consecration, and it is very definitely an internal problem. It does
raise the vexed issue of, What is a Jew? I, personally, accept the dictum of Paul, that "He is a Jew, which is one
inwardly; and circumcision is that of the heart, in the
spirit, and not in the letter; whose praise is not of men,
but of God."[2] The third part of the answer concerning
Jewish indirectness lies in the delicacy and gentleness
which Judaism inculcates as a principle of conduct in
human dealings. Judaism abhors bluster and blatancy. It
denounces ostentation, and Jesus did but forcefully echo
its sentiments that good should be done by stealth. "But
when thou bestowest alms, let not thy left hand know
what thy right hand doeth: that thine alms may be in

---

1 See Beales, *The Catholic Church and International Order*
   (Penguin Special).
2 *Rom.* ii. 29.

secret."[1] It is a maxim of the Rabbis that, "He who bestows alms in secret is greater than Moses our Teacher."[2]

The Jew is widely known for his generosity and willingness to extend the helping hand; but the teaching of Judaism is that in exercising this ministry he should keep out of the picture as far as possible lest he put his needy brother to an open shame. "Better is it for a man to fling himself into a fiery furnace than to cause his neighbour to blush in public."[3] It is thus more commendable for Jews to work for the welfare and progress of their fellow-men while keeping in the background, and avoiding any suggestion of Jewish hegemony or claiming merit as Jews.

It is difficult enough at times to preserve this principle inviolate. Jews are only human, and they do complain when they notice that it is often the way that when one of their number does something wrong he is described in print as a Jew. Whereas, when he does something fine or noble, he is described as an Englishman, Frenchman, or German, and the fact that he is a Jew is conveniently suppressed. He does resent the false impression thereby created, so that he gets all the kicks and precious few of the credits.

However, it is none the less his destiny to serve. The servant may be slandered, publicly vilified, and told he is good for nothing and the scum of the earth. Yet it is his

1 *Matt*. vi. 3-4.
2 *Baba Bathra*, 9b.
3 *Kethuboth*, 67b.

business to be silent, obedient, devoted to duty, ready, gentle, deft, and self-obliterating.

III

It has been a natural consequence of this elusiveness, this wearing of a coat of many colours, that ill-disposed persons have thereby been enabled to accuse the Jews of the most fantastic crimes—and to win credence for their libels—or to claim that Jewry was sponsoring at one and the same time mutually exclusive ideologies, that it was of set purpose both plutocratic and communistic. One could, in fact, believe anything about Jews that one wished. Friendly persons have also felt that they were almost completely in the dark, and have sincerely desired to know what Jews really stood for. Matters have not been improved by the fact that Jews themselves have found it exceedingly difficult to give a clear and convincing self-explanation. With many the process of losing or concealing identity had advanced so far that the sun of Judaism had sunk completely below their mental horizon. They were like a man who has assumed so many aliases that he is unsure of his real name. All that remained was a sub-conscious impulse, an urge to set the world to rights, which it was hard to explain or put into words. With others, they could say what their own views as Jews were, but would they be justified in saying that these were the Jewish views? They felt honestly compelled to be evasive, which made the situation all the more unsatisfactory. Like the wind that "bloweth where it listeth", so was everyone born of the Jewish spirit.

Judaism was not dogmatic: it was dynamic. It had its revelation and its ethic: it had its sublime objective; but it was so boundless in scope, so comprehensive, that you could take any progressive idea, any answer to the riddle of being, and quite correctly describe it as Jewish. Conversely, you could take anything retarding or harmful and say that it was un-Jewish.

Being mortal, and having finite minds like the rest of humanity, Jews have been worried not a little by the enigma of their faith—especially in modern times. It was rather different when they had no rights as citizens, no right to speak at all. They could be more speculative and less specialized then. But in an age which showed some adherence to the principles of liberty, equality, and fraternity there appeared no longer to be a necessity to remain wrapped in impenetrable mystery any more than to be confined within the walls of a Ghetto. Why now could not the pinions of Judaism be folded at last and come to rest on the historic plane instead of fluttering dazzlingly and indeterminately? Was there no contemporary point to which it could fittingly attach itself?

The result has been in some Jewish circles a revolt against anonymity. "We have done nothing as Jews for centuries," complains Strelitzki in *Children of the Ghetto*. "Cannot we be a conscious force making for nobler ends? Could we not, for instance, be the link of federation among the nations, acting everywhere in favour of peace? Could we not be the centres of new sociologic movements in each country?"

The revolt has taken different forms, in Liberal Judaism on the one hand and in Zionism on the other. Both are really aiming at Jewish self-explanation, and to provide opportunity for the intelligible fulfilment of the Jewish mission. They appear to be quite distinctive; but actually they are the opposite faces of the same coin.

It is foreign to the intention of this book to deal with either in any detail; but certain salient features are pertinent to this inquiry and could not be left out of account. They do help to clarify the present approach of Judaism to the problem of World Order.

Liberal Judaism is essentially the product of Jewish emancipation. It is an attempt, otherwise than through Christianity, to make of Judaism a world religion. In its external relations, therefore, it cannot help but contact Christianity at many points; it also has a kinship with the older Hellenistic Judaism.

Liberal Judaism takes its stand on the fundamental doctrine of Monotheism, and on the moral and ethical teachings of the Bible. These, it claims correctly enough, "are universal in character, and it is believed that the world will ultimately adopt them." It is argued that "there is a considerable number of Christians whose religious home seems nearer to Judaism than to Christianity", and that many of the festivals of the synagogue can become catholic and universal; "how they can be made to celebrate, how they actually do celebrate, certain broad human conceptions which are not limited by race or na-

tionality; how, finally, the holiest day of the Jewish cal-
endar is certainly also its most broadly and essentially
human holy day... in its independence of historic incid-
ent and in the universality of its appeal."[1]

Thus Jews, as Jews, can fulfil their mission: they can
consciously and openly assume spiritual leadership of
the nations. Judaism of this kind can become mission-
ary; it can propagate its faith abroad; it can advertise its
services in the press; it can, in short, establish a Church
of Moses and the Prophets.

Liberal Judaism tends to submerge, or at least sublim-
ate, Jewish nationalism, and does not therefore regard
Zionism with any favour. Yet the link between them may
perhaps be found in a statement by the Jewish writer,
Feuchtwanger, author of *Jew Suss*, in an article published in The Sentinel. "I am bold enough," he wrote, "to
dream further than the most ardent Zionist, to dream
that Jerusalem would become the centre not only of
Judaism, but of the whole world. Yes, when I am quite
bold, then I dream that Jerusalem might become for the
world what the founders of the League of Nations had
dreamed Geneva would become for all mankind."

There can be no doubt of the good work done by Liberal
Judaism in bringing the Biblical religions closer together
by promoting societies for Jews and Christians and so
fostering mutual understanding and co-operation in the

---

1 The quotations are from *The Place of Judaism among the
   Religions of the World,* by the late Dr. Claude G. Montefiore.

upholding of spiritual values in an increasingly secularist world.

Zionism, like Liberal Judaism, is a product of Jewish emancipation. It reflects in one aspect the rude awakening from the dear illusion that the new spirit of enlightenment abroad in the world of the nineteenth century necessarily meant the end of injustice and persecution for the Jew. Theodor Herzl, founder of Zionism, and others, faced with the fact that anti-semitism was still rife and virulent in almost every country in Europe, saw that until Jews could enjoy inalienable rights of citizenship secured to them in a state of their own they could never acquire that dignity in the eyes of the world which would lay the anti-semitic bogey. "It is a national question," he urged, "which can only be solved by making it a political world-question to be discussed and settled by the civilized nations of the world in council."[1]

Herzl continued: "We have honestly endeavoured everywhere to merge ourselves in the social life of surrounding communities and to preserve only the faith of our fathers. We are not permitted to do so. In vain are we loyal patriots, our loyalty in some places running to extremes; in vain do we make the same sacrifices of life and property as our fellow-citizens; in vain do we strive to increase the fame of our native land in science and art, or her wealth by trade and commerce. In countries where we have lived for centuries we are still cried down as strangers, and often by those whose ancestors were

---

1   *The Jewish State*, p. 15 (English Edition)

not yet domiciled in the land where Jews had already made experience of suffering."[1] The solution is the Jewish State.

"We are a people," announced Herzl; and Zionism declared the right of self-determination for peoples to apply also to the Jews, and linked this on to the age-old prophetic promise of the restoration of Israel to its native land.

We can be Jews again, we must be, Zionism cried, politically as well as religiously. Only so can we make any real world contribution.

Nationalism is regarded to-day increasingly as a hindrance to peaceful human relations, as a cause of friction and economic distress. How then can a rabid Jewish nationalism contribute to world progress and understanding? Has it not, in fact, in the Arab question in Palestine, sown the seeds of further discord? One cannot deny that in its regained national consciousness the Jewish people has not exhibited wisdom in the attitude of some of its elements. There has been, as well as a noble, sacrificial, regenerative, and idealistic expression, which has transformed Palestine, a certain amount of copying of the worst social and political features of other lands. These tendencies will no doubt disappear in time, and the Holy Land will exercise a sanctifying influence on its restored inhabitants.

---

1   Ibid.

There is the claim, however, widely acknowledged in current thought, that a spiritually-minded nation could lead the world into better ways. Jews want the chance to be that nation. As one of the New Zionists (or Revisionists) [1] has lately written: "We want to forget a study of geography which, in recent years, has made us experts on every unhealthy and hopeless corner of the globe, and explore our own land. We shall not stammer brokenly in the many languages our weary pilgrimage from one land to the next forces us to adopt, but concentrate on our own tongue and culture. And we want—since our wise men tell us that we have a 'mission'—to interpret this mission, not as an arrogant assumption of superiority which ill becomes a nation of hopeless beggars, but as the contribution to the sum of human progress which a people can only make when living free and secure on its own soil." [2]

The closing words of this quotation appeal to common sense. Quite apart from its being an act of historic justice to restore the Jewish people to its ancestral homeland, the Jew urgently needs a National Home—a home, if you will, in the sense of sanatorium, where he can recover from the mental shock of centuries of persecution, where he can regain his psychological balance, recuperate from the injuries inflicted upon him by the nations. Probably nowhere else than in the traditionally familiar and genial atmosphere of Palestine can this pathological treatment be fully efficacious. [3] If the Jew has a destiny of blessing

---

1   The absolutist national party.
2   Dr. Harry C. Schnur, in an article in *The Jewish Standard*, 1942.
3   One remembers how the shell-shocked and stricken soldiers of

to mankind to fulfil he can only carry it out as a sane and free man, when the experience of his sufferings will not unduly overshadow his life, but enrich it with a spirit of tolerance and compassion. In those circumstances, terrible as the price has been, anti-semitism may prove to have been the means of the world's salvation. Here again Judaism through Zionism nearly touches Christianity, for it was written of Jesus, "that he by the grace of God should taste death for every man. For it became God, for Whom are all things, and by Whom are all things, in bringing many sons unto glory, to make the captain of their salvation perfect through suffering."[1]

With the Exiles of Babylon of old the Jew may ask again to-day, "How shall we sing the Lord's song in a strange land?"[2] The fruits of national restoration may indeed realize the prophetic visions, and remove for ever the necessity for anonymity and indirect action in the Jewish striving for the welfare of humanity. The Holy Land, which has already been the means of giving such mighty and redemptive revelations of the Fatherhood of God and the Brotherhood of Man, may have its most stupendous and salutary revelation for men and nations yet in store.

---

the last war appropriately and half-humorously fitted to one of Sousa's marching tunes, the refrain, "You'll be far better off in a home".

1   *Hebrews* ii. 9-10.
2   *Psalm* cxxxvii. 4.

Chapter II

Negative Aspects

I

In all the long history of Jewish suffering there would seem to be no equal to the cumulative horrors of the past decade. The coming to power of Nazism, and all that has flowed from it in sheer brutality, has wrought such havoc among the Jewish people on the continent of Europe that it is doubtful if more than a very small proportion of those who are left there will survive this war.

Before 1939, in the great Democracies, Christian feeling was partly aroused to protest against this inhuman persecution and to give aid to the victims. That awakened conscience is still moderately active, but has had many other claims on its attention since the war began. Public opinion, however, has shown little concern for the fate of the Jews. Accounts of atrocities against them make news, but not headline news. Less injured peoples get the heavy type. One might be tempted, uncharitably, to think that the opponents of Nazism were secretly glad that there would be a good few thousand less Jews in the world.

Anti-semitism is certainly on the upgrade in many countries outside German control, and after the war the disease may spread further. There is every prospect of it. Nazism brackets Judaism with Democracy in its denunciations; but scarcely a single statesman among the United Nations dares to accept the challenge and boldly say that he is proud of the association, and means to stand by the Jews at any cost. Of course not: it would give far too much offence, and hinder the war effort.[1] A section of the Jewish people has even offered to raise and equip its own army to fight Nazism. In the U.S.A. large press advertisements have featured the offer. In Great Britain the project has the support of that inveterate champion of the Jews, Lord Wedgwood. But in official circles the plan is frowned upon. Other nationals are encouraged to have their own forces; but not the Jews: it would never do.

The plain fact is that all the world, not just the Nazis, brackets the Jews with what it fears and dislikes.

I do not favour the creation of a Jewish Army, though I can sympathize with those who do. The duties of a Jew as a citizen in serving with the Armed Forces are performed as a citizen, and not as a Jew. They could only be performed as a Jew if citizenship were of a Jewish State, as in the heroic past.

---

1   See, however, Appendix C.

But fighting will not save the Jew. It never has done, and never can. Judaism has been perpetuated through peace-seeking: its greatest victories have been won by non-violence.[1] The Jewish mission is essentially to be the Apostle of Peace, and the Jewish prayer is not for triumph over enemies, but that wars should cease from off the earth.[2] "Swords into plowshares" is the true Jewish Gospel. It is this *strength made perfect in weakness* that has been one of the means of the Jewish people's preservation. As Dr. Inge has written: "They have stood at the graveside of all their persecutors," and they have been enabled so to stand because they themselves lifted no carnal weapon against them.

This does not mean that the Jew is a physical weakling. His prowess in athletics, his hard navvying in Palestine, his record as a skilled pugilist, offer sufficient testimony to the contrary.

But it cannot be that a belligerent and militaristic people shall bring harmony and peace to a distracted world. It is written in the Scriptures: "Then David the king stood up upon his feet, and said, Hear me, my brethren, and my people: As for me, I had in mine heart to build an house of rest for the ark of the covenant of the Lord, and for the footstool of our God, and had made ready for the building; But God said unto me, Thou shalt not build an house for My Name, *because thou hast been a man of war, and hast shed blood....* And He said unto, me, So-

---

1   Cf. Josephus, *Antiq.*, bk. xviii. chs. 3 and 8.
2   See above.

lomon (the *Peaceable*) thy son, he shall build My house and My courts: for I have chosen him to be My son, and I will be his Father."[1] Nevertheless, the Jews to-day are greatly tempted—almost beyond endurance. Faced acutely with the problem of self-preservation in an age supremely hostile to them, it requires superlative moral courage not to resort to force. Yet if they should lack this courage they are lost indeed, and the hope of mankind would be buried in the ruins of their fall.

In concluding his book on *The Jewish Problem*,[2] my friend Louis Golding used some very brave words:

> "There is another knowledge we bear with us," he wrote, "some of us obscurely, too deep for words, some of us clearly; and we render it in word or sound or stone. It is not only that we need each other, but that the world needs us. We have stood since our beginnings for certain values, which the world would cherish without us, but with us cherishes more bravely and continuously. We have stood for the idea of One God, for Peace throughout the Lands, for Love to All Men. The treatment of us is a touchstone of a land's chivalry. Where things are well with us, there the newer values flourish, Religious Liberty, Democracy, the Right of Free Speech. Where things go ill, these values sicken, and soon after, those older values follow.
>
> "The world needs us. We cannot fail each other. We will go on."

---

1   I *Chron.* xxviii. 2-6.
2   P. 213.

That passage was written in 1938. Things were bad then, but they have since become incredibly worse. Perhaps Golding could still write as bravely. I do not know, and I do not dare to ask him. "We will go on!" Not many Jews could say that with any assurance to-day.

II

Throughout its chequered past the Jewish people has been amazingly optimistic. It has believed implicitly in its own future and in human progress. From this spiritual confidence it has drawn the strength to surmount its sufferings and misfortunes: it has had the will to live.

When the Jews were the victims of the "Crusade against Mohammedanism", and the ribald and fanatical soldiery butchered thousands of men, women, and children in the cities of the Rhineland on their way to deliver the Holy Sepulchre, Jewish courage partly failed. Their prayers for help were answered then by the timely appearance and preaching of St. Bernard of Clairvaux. "If our Creator in His great compassion had not sent us this abbot," wrote a Jewish contemporary, "there would have been none in Israel that would have escaped or remained alive. Blessed be He who saves and delivers. Praised be His Name."[1]

But in the Middle Ages, at least, the Jews had learnt to accept insult and ignominy as their portion. It is other-

---

1   Ephraim of Bonn, 1180.

wise in these days of reputed civilization in which liberal ideas and principles of individual freedom have flourished. Though hatred and persecution might continue, there was every hope of betterment and the ultimate repudiation of intolerance. Across the seas the United States of America was offering a haven to the oppressed. Jewish gratitude penned the words engraved upon the Statue of Liberty in New York Harbour:

> "Not like the brazen giant of Greek fame,
> With conquering limbs astride from land to land;
> Here at our sea-washed, sunset gates shall stand
> A mighty woman with a torch whose flame
> Is the imprisoned lightning, and her name
> Mother of Exiles. From the beacon-hand
> Blows world-wide welcome; her mild eyes command
> The air-bridged harbor that twin cities frame.
> 'Keep, ancient lands, your storied pomp!' cries she
> With silent lips. 'Give me your tired, your poor,
> Your huddled masses yearning to breathe free,
> The wretched refuse of your teeming shore.
> Send these, the homeless, tempest-tossed, to me;
> I lift up my lamp beside the golden door!'"[1]

By comparison, therefore, the shock of the present catastrophe has been far more overwhelming. The modern Jewish victims of the so-called "Crusade against Bolshevism" are even more despairing. The vileness, the

---

1   *The New Colossus*, by Emma Lazarus.

tortures and massacres perpetrated by the Nazi soldiery and S. S. Guards, who class all who stand in their path as "Jews and Communists", coupled with the almost universal spread of the anti-semitic poison, has rudely shaken Jewish faith. Appalled by the fate of their co-religionists in Europe; shocked beyond measure at the crash of twentieth-century civilization; the Jewish people is in danger of losing the will to live, of surrendering its faith in man as made in the image of God. Jewish suicides have become all too frequent, and a chill pessimism has set in. Can one any more credit that there can ever be a New World Order?

Jews do not stand alone in viewing with despair the calamity of two world wars in a quarter of a century, the outbreak of a ruthless spirit of aggression and domination, the evidence of the bestialities of which modern man is capable, the indifference to the taking of life and the destruction of culture. Many people have become sceptical, cynical, and misanthropic. Not all the Atlantic Charters, Four Freedoms, or Principles of Social Justice, convey any impression of reality. They look forward with dismal foreboding to an era of anarchy, followed perhaps by a third world war a quarter of a century hence. Who that has lived through these times can honestly blame them?

Made incredibly sensitive by their afflictions the Jews have developed into a human barometer, faithfully recording the changes in world conditions. Just now that barometer shows a heavy fall. The needle has swung right over.

Yet hope springs eternal. God has not forsaken His creation. "Plan, plan, plan," drums out the message of the heart and mind. "We have destroyed; we can rebuild. We have failed; we can yet succeed." Judaism is greater than the Jew, greater than the Gentile. God's Kingdom will come on earth at last.

III

Defeat, spiritual defeat, for the people which beyond all others exemplifies the verity of an eternal purpose for mankind, has in this period been a very near thing. The world, if it but knew the momentous significance of the crisis, ought to be hanging breathless on the issue—not of who will win the war, that is but a ghastly episode, but of whether the Jew will survive and recover, whether he will regain his faith in the Love of God and the Brotherhood of Man. Only if the Jew wins through will life and history be meaningful again.

Just now the Jew has been driven back on the second line of his defences. His traditional safeguards have been abandoned. Pathetically he pleads for justice to a generation which has made a mockery of justice; but even that plea is weakening. Implacable faces ring the Jew on every side.

Before the situation became aggravated, public opinion was already growing tired of the Jewish clamour for its rights, its Protest Meetings, its Defence Committees, its Congressional claims for repatriation and protection secured by International Law and Treaty. There was something pitiful, and rather disgusting, in the Jewish fawning on highly placed Gentile friends, the lavish adulation of those who would speak a favourable word. There was the impression that Jews were making far too much of their undoubted tribulations, and there was a tendency to discount much of what was reported as exaggerated propaganda. Anyway, if they had to suffer, why could they not do it with dignity and decency, like "Christians"?

Who could guess that really it was the world's soul that was in travail, crying out through Jewish lips, and waiting to be delivered?

But it was unhealthy, this obsession with self, as is sometimes the condition of a pregnant woman, who becomes plaintive, self-pitying, demanding, and egocentric. And similarly it was largely the product of a nervously fearful and unbalanced state. Sheer panic, an end-of-all-things complex, had the Jewish spirit in its grip. Faith and reason alike could not reassert themselves, and bring conviction that this trial too would be overpassed, unprecedented though it might seem and hard to endure.

This has been the Jewish failure—an understandable one, but no less deplorable. If in this grave hour of decision the Jews could have risen to the sublime heights of self-abnegation, if they could have unitedly externalized their thoughts, setting themselves to concentrate on caring for others, working as a body quietly, efficiently, and unflinchingly to minister to the world's needs, they might have won the approbation and love of mankind, and a new day would have dawned. If the Jewish people, with its international character, could have convened a Sanhedrin not to discuss the problems of Jews or the fate of Jews, but—according to the wise and beneficent principles of Judaism—to deal faithfully with the manifold problems and disorders of men and nations, and published their findings to the world, they might have succeeded in doing what neither the League of Nations nor its Permanent Court of International Justice could accomplish. *It is still not too late.*

Individual Jews have made a wonderful and impressive contribution, but not primarily as a Jewish contribution. Nothing less than a collective contribution as Jews will suffice. True, the effort might fail; the revolt of man against spiritual guidance might appear to destroy its efficacy. But it would be a glorious failure, and if it brought martyrdom it would also prove to be the seed of ultimate salvation. The responsibility for the intervening setback would rest with man, not with the Jews.

I believe that this is the Jewish mission, though the manner of its execution be different from what Jews have imagined in recent times. Yet it is wholly in line with what the Jewish seers of old had visioned.

I believe that only a consecrated nation can mediate between the nations. No other body, religious or secular, will serve.[1]

I believe that sincere Christians and other men of goodwill would associate themselves with such a lead. Old wounds would be healed, and the ends of the earth would break forth into a new song of harmony.

Thus the solution of what Golding rightly calls "the Gentile Problem" would have solved for ever the Jewish Problem, and the brand of Cain would be erased from the forehead of Homo Sapiens. For—let everyone earnestly consider—how can there be peace and happiness while hatred for a single individual, much more a whole people, endures?[2] The final disappearance of anti-semitism is therefore the test of the worth of all human professions of amity. So long as it exists anywhere there can be no righteous World Order. To achieve that good thing both Jews and Gentiles must play their part. Yet even if neither should rise to their great opportunity, does that mean that the Messianic Hope of Judaism will not be

---

1 The British Israelites, who believe in Britain's divine mission and have little to do with Jews, would endorse this statement.
2 The alternative is a perpetuation of Nazism, over which Professor Kittel rejoiced when it came to power in 1933. "A new movement, full of life," he wrote, "has broken out in our midst, to which not world citizenship and universal culture is the ideal, but a culture bound up with the people.... What it can contribute in spiritual values it can give best by developing its own inherent culture, which springs from blood and soil, *and by killing as poison all that opposes it*" (Italics are mine).—*Die Judenfrage.*

realized, that the noble desires which that faith has im-
planted in the hearts of men will remain unfulfilled?

Chapter III

Has Judaism a Programme?

I

I concluded the previous chapter with a question, and I have headed this one with another. To answer them both it will be necessary in some measure to divorce Judaism from the Jewish people. This may appear difficult when Judaism has been regarded as the religion of a people, and Jews as the people of a religion. But it is not impossible.

I have admitted that as yet, except for the Zionist aspect, the Jewish people *per se* has no programme, which could be construed as a constructive design for a New World Order. Neither, of course, as is falsely represented by its enemies, has it any design for World Dominion to the detriment of non-Jews.

The Jewish people has no *Sword of the Spirit Movement*. It has created no *Commission for International Friendship and Social Responsibility*. It has issued no *Peace Points*. It has initiated none of these and similar activities as have the Christian Churches. This does not mean that Jews have been indifferent to the burning problems of our time. There are in existence, mainly in the United States, Jewish Peace Societies, Study Groups, and Research Committees, which are doing a valuable work of investigation. A list of such organizations has been published recently in the directory of the Geneva Research Centre. Individual Jews are prominent in most non-Jewish associations for world betterment.

But, on the other hand, how much of the motivating power behind the present Christian proclamation of a Social Gospel is directly due to Judaism?

Here is what an eminent Roman Catholic writer has said:

> "From the first Israel appears to us a mystery; of the same order as the mystery of the world and the mystery of the Church.... Between Israel and the world, as between the Church and the world, there is a supra-human relation. It is only by considering this triad, that one can form some idea, even enigmatically, of the mystery of Israel.... The communion of this mystical body is the communion of mundane hope. Israel passionately hopes, waits, yearns for the coming of God on earth, the kingdom of *God here below*. With an eternal will, a supernatural and non-rational will, it desires justice in time, in nature, and in the cities of man.... Israel, we believe, is assigned a task of *earthly activization* of the mass of the world. Israel, which is not of

the world, is to be found at the very heart of the world's structure, stimulating it, exasperating it, moving it. Like an alien body, like an activating leaven injected into the mass, it gives the world no peace, it bars slumber, it teaches the world to be discontented and restless as long as the world has not God; it stimulates the movement of history."[1]

In embarking on its new campaigns for international political and social justice the Church, more than it knows or realizes, has been reconverted to Judaism. The revival of the theocratic principle of human government is indeed one of the major signs of the times. Stanley Jones is surely right in affirming: "As the demand for an all-comprehending principle and power for unity is now pressing upon the world-soul, this buried idea of the Kingdom of God is becoming a new, living issue. It is experiencing nothing less than a resurrection, and is becoming the question of questions."[2]

During the nineteenth century the Christian emphasis lay elsewhere. It was directing the oppressed masses into an escapist religion alien to Jewish doctrine: it was filling their mouths, not with bread, but with songs of a blessed hereafter to mitigate the crushing misery of their earthly lot. They were taught to sing of Beulah Land and Immanuel's Land, which had no connection with the prophetic vision of a regenerated Palestine. They were told to look forward eagerly to crossing a Jordan, which required no physical ford or ferry, in order to be sure of

---

1   Jacques Maritain, *Anti-Semitism,* pp. 17-20.
2   *Christ and Present World Issues,* p. 17.

arriving at some celestial *There* "when the roll is called up yonder". No wonder that the revolutionary social reformers described such religion contemptuously as "dope".

It has taken a cataclysmic upheaval of society, and the upsurging of an anti-Christian spirit, to restore in large part to the Councils of the Church the faith of its original Jewish Apostles.

Christianity is nearer to Judaism to-day than it has been in eighteen centuries. It is coming back home. It is returning to its Jewish parent, like the Prodigal Son to his Father's house; and Judaism should welcome this restoration with the same joyous greeting: "This my son was dead, and is alive again; he was lost, and is found."[1]

Judaism does not ask Christianity to abandon its creed as the price of reconciliation, or for a penitent acknowledgment of faults. It makes no terms. But it does ask, and has a right to ask, that in future the relationship should be publicly acknowledged in word and deed, that the family circle should not again be broken by a "journey into a far country" which has had such bitter consequences, that the son shall not be ashamed of the old Jew with his foreign ways and bundle him into a back room out of sight when visitors call. Otherwise, if the son shall give himself airs,[2] and go off again, and there is

---

1 *Luke* xv. 24. The whole parable is worthy of re-reading from this viewpoint.
2 Parochialism is still a limiting factor in Church life. It needs the universal international outlook of Judaism.

another "famine in that land"—a famine of the word of God—and he "shall begin to be in want," he may return too late, and find his father—dead.

Only by the close co-operation of Christianity and Judaism as kinsmen, can the peril in which humanity stands to-day be averted. As in the parable it is up to the son to make the first move; but be sure the father will by no means await his arrival: he will run to meet him.

II

It may not yet be apparent how infused with the Ethics of Judaism are the policies which are now being so strongly advocated by the Churches. I therefore propose to quote somewhat fully an article on Jewish ethics written about forty years ago, and which on that account cannot be represented as reflecting the recent conclusions of Christian Conferences. The article is by the late Rabbi E.G. Hirsch of Chicago, and will be found in Volume V of the Jewish Encyclopaedia. I have space here only for the final section:

> "The ethical teachings of religion alone, and especially the Jewish religion, establish the relation of man to himself, to his property, to others, on an ethical basis. Religion sets forth God as the Giver. Non-religious ethics is incompetent to develop consistently the obligations of man to live so that the measure of his life, and the value and worth of all other men, shall be increased. Why should man not be selfish? Why is Nietzsche's 'overman', who

is 'beyond good and evil', not justified in using his strength as he lists? Religion, and it alone, or a religious interpretation of ethics makes the social bond something more comprehensive than an accidental and natural (material) compact between men, a policy, a prudential arrangement to make life less burdensome; religion alone makes benevolence and altruism something loftier than mere anticipatory speculations on possible claims for benefits when necessity shall arise, or the reflex impulse of a subjective transference of another's objective misery to oneself, so that pity always is shown only to self (Schopenhauer). Religion shows that as man is the recipient of all he is and has, he is the steward of what was given to him (by God) for his use and that of all his fellow men.

"On this basis of Jewish ethics rests its doctrines of duty and virtue. Whatever increases the capacity of man's stewardship is ethical. Whatever use of time, talent, or treasure augments one's possibilities of human service is ethically consecrated. Judaism, therefore, inculcates as ethical the ambition to develop physical and mental powers, as enlargement of service is dependent upon the measure of the increase of man's powers. Wealth is not immoral; poverty is not moral. The desire to increase one's stores of power is moral provided it is under the consecration of the recognized responsibility for larger service. The weak are entitled to the protection of the strong. Property entails duties, which establish its rights. Charity is not a voluntary concession on the part of the well-situated. It is a right to which the less fortunate are entitled in justice (*Tsedakah*). The main concern of Jewish ethics is personality. Every human being is a person, not a thing. Economic doctrine is unethical and un-Jewish if it ignores and renders illusory this distinction. Slavery is for this reason immoral. Jewish ethics on this basis is not individualistic it is not under the spell of otherworldliness. It is social. By consecrating every human being to the stewardship of his faculties and forces, and by regarding every human soul as a person, the ethics of Judaism offers the solution of all the perplexities of modern political, industrial, and economic life. Israel as the 'pattern people' shall be exponential, among its brothers of the whole human family, of the principles and practices which are involved in, pillared upon, and demanded by, the ethical monotheism which lifts man to the dignity of God's image and consecrates him the steward of all of his life, his talent, and his treasure. In the 'Messianic kingdom', ideally to be anticipated by Israel, justice will be enthroned and incarnated in institution, and this justice, the social correlative of holiness and love, is the ethical passion of modern, as it was of olden, Judaism."

The above extract will perhaps clarify further the position of Judaism, and reveal the common foundation upon which Church and Synagogue are now standing.

But when we are thinking of a programme we are thinking of more than fundamental principles and ethics.

Judaism has a programme, laid down in its sacred literature, and it is a far-reaching one, to which also Christianity must be a party, and towards the accomplishment of which it must be a working partner. A clue to its nature is found in the phrase quoted above, "Israel as the pattern people

Conscious to-day of the supreme need for a Christian example to be shown to the world, of the reality of a loyalty higher than that due to any human agency, the Church is turning back to Judaism in another connection.

Primitive Christianity was aware of its independent nationhood, in a literal sense. It regarded itself as the New Israel, inheritor of the mission of its Jewish ancestors, "a chosen race, a royal priesthood, an holy nation, a peculiar people... which in time past were not a people, but were now the people of God".[1]

Eusebius, the fourth-century Church historian, stated explicitly: "It is evident, that but a short time after the appearance of our Saviour Jesus Christ had been made known to all men, a new nation suddenly came into existence; a nation confessedly neither small nor weak, nor situated in a remote corner of the earth, but the most populous and religious of all, and so much the more indestructible and invincible as it has always had the power of God as its support. This nation, appearing at

---

1   1 *Peter* ii. 9-10.

the time appointed by inscrutable wisdom, is that which among all is honoured with the name of Christ."[1]

This awareness of distinct nationhood, which lately has again become current in certain Christian circles, goes back directly to the doctrine of Judaism, which declared of Israel "Ye shall be unto Me a kingdom of priests, and an holy nation."[2]

Judaism is not disposed at this late and critical epoch to enter into the controversy as to which community is the true nation, the true people of God. Why, in fact, should the two not be one? There is room within the framework of such nationhood for complete freedom of conscience and worship. It could not be otherwise. What is vital for building a New World Order is the objective purpose of such a nation.

There can be no doubt that Jews and Christians are being brought together again in a surprising, and I would not hesitate to say Providential, way. Mutually fortifying each other in a common world citizenship, they could indeed show forth the exemplification of a "pattern people", on the basis of moral force, social justice, and corporate service.

If this is the Divine Plan, nothing can resist its fulfilment. And so our questions are answered.

---

1   *Eccles. Hist.*, bk. iv. ch. i.
2   *Exod.* xix. 6. See above, pp. 23-26.

Chapter IV

The Holy Nation and World Order

I

Granting that both Judaism and Chritianity envisage the redemption of the world through the agency of a Holy Nation, how may this idea be associated with present tendencies and needs?

In a last attempt at escape from the perpetuation of conflict between nations the despairing mind of man has indicted the concept of sovereignty as being the real obstacle to the settlement of disputes among peoples by peaceful means. It is argued that the relinquishment of certain powers of the nation-states to a Federal Government, League of Nations Council, or other International Authority, would remove not only the necessity for war, but the means to prosecute it—independent armed forces.

The fallacy of this reasoning should be evident, if on no other grounds than its failure to touch psychological issues. A mixed League or Federation is bound to break down on matters more fundamental than the actual excuse for defection. What in fact these expedients propose, as man's best safeguard against international anarchy, is that groups of Powers, which already have much in common, should loosely (Confederation) or closely (Federation) coalesce so as to create more formidable units. Far from stopping war this plan would be likely to breed others more terrible, because more co-ordinated.

But these policies do have the excellence of recognizing the need for self-sacrifice in the interests of a wider harmony. It is not the fault of the policies that they also have the fatal quality of failing to provide a bridge between incompatible ideologies. They are Tower of Babel solutions, built on the foundation of collective security. What we can say of these proposed national groupings is that they would narrow down the field of mediation. But an entirely disinterested mediatorial agency there must be.

It is not really national sovereignty that is at the root of the conflict: it is the spiritual condition of humanity. National sovereignty is a protection against universal tyranny, and will so remain until there exists a true brotherhood of man arising out of the common recognition of the sovereignty of God. His is the only world dominion that is not domination.

What at least has already emerged out of the welter of strife in line with God's purposes is the aim at world community and world citizenship, which is featured in both League of Nations and Federal Union propaganda. It is seen that there must be a loyalty above that which is due from subjects to their own nation-state. The more constructive of political thinkers are emphasizing it. I may quote two of many similar expressions of opinion.

"The world community," writes Prof. G. M. Stratton, "is in need of its own form of loyalty. Without this the world can never become a governed body."[1]

Dr. L.P. Jacks says further: "Were there in existence a universal Church in which men of all races and ways of thinking could find their spiritual home, and unite in one fellowship of loyalty and goodwill, it would be unquestionably the world's most valuable institution."[2]

Let us multiply by all means the number of practicable and non-conflicting international organizations, and let us in every possible way educate our children in the principles upon which true world community can be founded, but let us no less frankly realize that the governmental union of all nations is still far distant, and that therefore it offers no immediate or even near solution to our problems. What we have to concern ourselves with is the bridge that will bring us safely to that farther shore. And in considering this bridge we must also con-

---

1   *International Delusions,* p. 197.
2   *Co-operation or Coercion?,* p. 90.

sider that the goal of our hope cannot be a new Babel, which apparently would satisfy many, a Cosmopolis in which all human viciousness would agglomerate: it must be a Theopolis, a City of God, in which there can be no place for lying and duplicity. The character of this goal should alone be sufficient to show us how remote we are from it.

In the faith of Judaism and Christianity this bridge is called the Kingdom of God, and the builders of the bridge are called the People of God.

It is here that the pattern comes in, the power of example. As Seneca has said: "Men trust rather to their eyes than to their ears; the effect of precepts is therefore slow and laborious, whilst that of examples is summary and effectual." To hope to bring order into international chaos by moral persuasion, by high-sounding phrases of covenant and treaty, by declarations of rights and the passing of legislation, if not entirely futile, is at least an expectation that depends on a protracted process. Neither men nor nations are readily made good by law. Only by demonstrating in an actual nation the ability to live up to the laws of God, showing what a people should be in all its relations, will others be transformed by that example.

The thought of example, as applied to nations, is not foreign to contemporary political ideas. It is often suggested that Britain or the United States, as wealthy and influential Powers, should "give a lead". Unfortunately, like the rich young ruler of the gospel story, they are unequal to the demand, and hold back from Messianic service because of their great possessions. "The world must have a solemn, clear, simple word from Great Britain," writes Salvador de Madariaga. "The nation of the King's peace, the fatherland of self-government, must say to the world: I BELIEVE IN THE WORLD COMMONWEALTH. That is all that is wanted."[1] Alas, it is not so simple as that. The chill fact has to be faced that the World Commonwealth is at present intangible and almost mythical. The nation-state is real to us: the world-state is unreal. We, therefore, have no sense of obligation and loyalty to what is imaginary.

Madariaga is more helpful in proposing as immediate aims "To organize on a world basis all that works on a world basis."[2] He thinks of the League, the International Labour Office and the World Court, of a World Bank and of a possible World Trade Commission. Very well. But none of these institutions affords a bridge between the nation-state and the world-state, though they may be sturdy piles driven into the bed of the river which we have to cross. We need some world-national framework which can be laid upon them, and which they will support; for between the two extremes of nation-state and world-state there must be an institution which partakes of the character of both.

---

1   *The World's Design*, p. 249.
2   *Ibid.*, p. 250.

The Divine Plan for the intermediate form of government is the only one that can prove efficacious, for it
provides an institution at once national and international. There comes into being a new nation with its own
citizenship, which yet being world-diffused, supra-territ-
orial, and inter-racial, represents a world citizenship.

II

The world needs the Holy Nation not only to act as a
bridge and a pattern of nationhood, but as a mediator.

Conspicuous among the deficiencies in our international
system is the lack of any impartial world authority capable of administering international law and exercising
functions of mediation and trusteeship. How grievously
to-day is felt that lack! Look where you will in other human relationships there is provision for appeal by dis-
putants to a mutually accepted third party, a
disinterested arbitrator. Only the nation-states have
found no such authority to serve them, for there is no
one outside of themselves, no external body which can
justly claim at the councils of nations, "We speak as the
guardians of the rights of man." The best machinery
hitherto devised is no more than an unsatisfying com-
promise.

The creation of an impartial and disinterested world authority is seen to be vital. It is required, among other
functions:

i. To stand above all races and religions, parties, classes, and ideologies.

ii. To give expression to the idea of world unity and the mutual interdependence of states.

iii. To act as the recorder man in his spiritual, physical, and social development.

iv. To act as the advocate of man in all that pertains to his rights, responsibilities, and corporate relationships.

v. To furnish a pattern of living based on the principles of love and service.

vi. To foster and promote education, experiment, and research for the benefit of all men everywhere.

vii. To act as trustee for all discoveries and inventions useful and necessary for the welfare of humanity.

viii. To act as guardian of minorities and backward races.

ix. To act as custodian and administrator of international law.

x. To provide a disinterested and impartial tribunal for the purposes of international mediation and arbitration.

xi. To form a bridge, and the mechanism of gradual transition, from the nation-state to the world-state.

xii. Generally to assume such powers as may be delegated by the freewill of all nations.

Such are only a few of the functions which an Impartial World Authority could perform. It necessitates absolute and inviolable neutrality, a representation of all mankind and a coverage of the whole globe. It excludes at once any league of nations, except of all nations, or any federation of states, except of all states. It excludes no less any attitude or philosophy, any religious or political concept, which outlaws, hereticizes, or deprives of common rights and security, any race, faith, class, or stratum of society, or any individuals composing the human brotherhood. It involves an interpenetration, both vertical and horizontal, so as to make representation real and understanding.

The World Authority must have a profound moral basis: it would be unacceptable without a widespread recognition of its righteousness. Self-denying service, justice, and benevolence, must be the keynotes of its character. It must have the spiritual power to evoke a responsive goodwill and bring out the best in men and nations.

The World Authority must be completely detached, free, and untrammelled. It must be able to establish and maintain itself as a sacred institution independent of the vicissitudes of states and empires. There can be no question of any of its members owning allegiance to any of the nation-states: they must have their own nationality, a universally accepted passport. It must have a clear constitution, which, while it demonstrates its uniqueness and defines its special status, makes it also the peer of the nation-states. This is necessary, not only for the usage of diplomatic machinery, but also to retain the sound principle of judgment by peers.

Such an Authority is the logical outcome of the aspirations of Judaism, and its age-old conception of a holy ministering nation. It offers the only valid solution to the problems which the world faces to-day.

III

If it should now be asked how such a desirable world authority and holy nation could come into being, one can say that between them the Jewish people and the Christian Church have all the essential qualifications. The most consecrated elements in both could easily combine to achieve it. With them would be associated a number of devoted people with a world-outlook who are adherents of other faiths. The "man without a country", the stateless person, would in this new national context become a title of honour, signifying a deliberate surrender of state protection and privilege for the sake of humanity. The

Holy Nation would be a microcosm, symbolical of world
unity, and capable of expansion not by might but by service until the ultimate World Commonwealth was
achieved.

Is this the real answer to domination and aggression, a
dienstvolk (servant-nation) instead of a *herrenvolk*
(master-nation)? Is this the new revelation for which
mankind has waited and prayed for in the hour of its
direst need? Or is this just another utopian dream, born
of the ancient Jewish prophetic spirit?

I can say that there exists already in England a Society
for the Constitution of a Holy Nation, with a growing following of Jews, Christians, and others. In Esperanto, invented by a Jew, there is a recognized world auxiliary
language suitable for such a nation to make its own.

If this plan, which has the will of God stamped upon it, is
not to be realized, what else will give us World Order?

Appendix A

World Benefactors of Jewish Faith or Heritage

This list is necessarily greatly abbreviated. Many famous Jews of world reputation in the Arts and Sciences, Politics and Commerce, have been excluded, while others whose names are little known have been given a place because of the benefits which mankind has derived from their work.

Ancient (in chronological order)

Moses..............................The Ten Commandments laid the foundation of society.

David..............................His Psalms have been the continual solace of humanity.

Isaiah..............................The prophet, whose vision of world peace and international order has been an incentive and inspiration to mankind.

Jesus...............................The Sermon on the Mount set the ideal standard of conduct, towards the attainment of which men have ceaselessly striven.

Paul.................................Promoted the brotherhood of man by proclaiming the Unity of God to the nations and universalizing the message of Judaism.

Maimonides....................Helped to unite East and West by his philosophic speculations.

Modern (in alphabetical order)

Adler, Felix.....................Founder of the Ethical Movement.

Barnardo, Dr...................Established   the   world's greatest orphanage.

Bergson, Henri.................Propounder of the Theory of Creative Evolution.

Blioch, Ivan.....................His proposals were responsible for the Hague Peace Conference of 1899 and the establishment of the Hague Tribunal for International Arbitration.

Curie, Mme......................Pioneer of Radio-therapy.

Durkheim, Emile..............Founder of Modern Sociology.

Ehrlich, Paul....................Discoverer of Salvarsan for the treatment of Venereal Diseases.

Einstein, Albert...............Author of the Theory of Relativity.

Freud, Sigismund............Discoverer of the Unconscious. Pioneer of Psycho-analysis.

Gomperz, Lewis...............Father of the Royal Society for the Prevention of Cruelty to Animals.

Herschel, Sir Wm............Discoverer of the Planet Uranus. One of the founders of Sidereal Science.

Hertz, Heinrich...............Discoverer of the Hertzian Waves, the basis of Wireless Telegraphy.

Koller, Carl.....................To whom is due the use of Cocaine as an anaesthetic.

Lasalle, Ferdinand...........Founder of Social Democracy.

Lippmann, Gabriel..........Inventor of Colour Photography.

Litvinov, Maxim..............Outstanding defender of the League of Nations.

Lombroso, Cesare...........Founder of the Science of Criminology. Pioneer of curative treatment for criminals.

Marx, Karl......................Father of Modern Communism.

Minkowski, Oscar............Whose researches contributed to the invention of Insulin for the treatment of Diabetes.

Phillips, L. B..................Inventor of the Keyless Watch.

Singer, Isaac...................Developed the Sewing Machine.

Spinoza, Benedict............One of the founders of Modern Philosophy and Liberal Thought.

Strauss, Nathan...............To whom was mainly responsible the introduction of Pasteurized Milk.

Traube, Ludwig...............Discoverer of Digitalin.

Valobra, Samson.............Inventor, of the Safety Match.

Van Praagh, William.......Pioneer of lip-reading for deaf-mutes.

Zamenhof, Lazar............Inventor of the auxiliary language of Esperanto.

Appendix B

Statement of Council of Christians and Jews

The Council of Christians and Jews was formed as a result of informal consultations which took place early in 1942 between representative leaders of the Jewish and Christian communities. Faced with a rising tide of anti-semitism in a world in which forces are at work which threaten to undermine the foundations both of Judaism and Christianity, those who were a party to these informal consultations felt that an organization was needed which should be as widely representative as possible of all interests in both communities and which should be able to concern itself not merely with the combating of racial and religious intolerance but also with the building up of such understanding and goodwill between Jews and Christians as would enable them to cooperate effectively in the furtherance of those principles which are common to both their religious traditions, always on the basis of mutual respect for the differences which exist between them.

A Statement embodying the considerations which had led to the formation of the Council, together with its aims,

was published at the beginning of October in the
following terms:

> "The following Statement is issued by the Arch-
> bishop of Canterbury, the Moderator of the Gen-
> eral Assembly of the Church of Scotland, the
> Moderator of the Free Church Federal Council, and
> the Chief Rabbi of the United Hebrew Congrega-
> tions of the British Empire—
>
> "The present German Government has consistently
> attempted to undermine and destroy those tradi-
> tional religious and spiritual values of mankind in
> which it recognizes its most dangerous enemies.
> The course of the war has seen a steady intensifica-
> tion of these attempts, and German conquests have
> enormously extended the area in which these
> policies can be ruthlessly applied.
>
> "In the forefront of their efforts to create division
> within every community the Nazis have always
> placed antisemitism, which is repugnant to the
> moral principles common to Christianity and
> Judaism alike. We cannot afford to ignore the ef-
> fects of the steady propagation of this evil through-
> out the world. It is not only a menace to the unity
> of every community in which it takes root, but it is
> the very negation of those values on which alone
> we believe that a new and better world can be es-
> tablished.
>
> "In these circumstances we are agreed that it
> would be for the general benefit to form in this
> country a Council of Christians and Jews, which
> might draw to itself the support in this matter of all

men and women of goodwill. Such a Council has now been formed and, as its joint Presidents, we have been gratified by the influential and whole-hearted response which has been immediately forthcoming.

"The aims of the Council are:

(a) To check and combat religious and racial intolerance.

(b) To promote mutual understanding and good-will between Christians and Jews in all sections of the community, especially in connection with problems arising from conditions created by the war.

(c) To promote fellowship between Christian and Jewish youth organizations in educational and cultural activities.

(d) To foster co-operation of Christians and Jews in study and service directed to post-war reconstruction.

"Further details will be announced in due course, and in the meantime inquiries should be addressed to the Hon. Secretaries, The Council of Christians and Jews, 21 Bloomsbury Street, London, W. C. 1.

"His Eminence Cardinal Hinsley, Archbishop of Westminster, endorses the condemnation of anti-semitism, and has, since the composition of this Statement, joined the Council as a Joint-President as a mark of his strong protest against all persecution of the Jewish People."

It may be added to their great credit that the Churches represented are doing their utmost to carry out the aims defined by the Statement.

Appendix C

Treatment of Jews: United Nations' Declaration (December 17, 1942)

Facts about Hitler's declared policy to exterminate the

Jews in Europe have now at last been sufficiently revealed. On 2nd December the U. S. State Department published a list of Jewish victims in Axis-controlled countries. Later, on 9th December, a statement was made in Great Britain in the House of Lords by the Archbishop of York. This was followed, on 17th December, by a Declaration of the United Nations issued simultaneously in London, Washington and Moscow. Much of the evidence had been collected by the Polish Government. The text of the Declaration, as read by Mr. Anthony Eden, the Foreign Secretary, to the House of Commons was as follows:

> "The attention of the Governments of Belgium, Czechoslovakia, Greece, Luxemburg, the Netherlands, Norway, Poland, U. S. A., United Kingdom, the U.S.S.R. and Yugoslavia, and the French Na-

tional Committee, has been drawn to numerous reports from Europe that the German authorities, not content with denying to persons of Jewish race in all territories over which their barbarous rule has been extended the most elementary human rights, are now carrying into effect Hitler's oft-repeated intention of exterminating the Jewish people in Europe. From all the occupied countries Jews are being transported in conditions of appalling horror and brutality to Eastern Europe.

"In Poland, which has been made the principal Nazi slaughterhouse, the ghettoes established by the German invader are being systematically emptied of all Jews except a few highly skilled workers required for war industry.

"None of those taken away are ever heard of again.

"The able-bodied are slowly worked to death in labour camps. The infirm are left to die of exposure and starvation or deliberately massacred in mass executions. The number of victims of these bloody murders is reckoned in many hundreds of thousands of entirely innocent men, women and children.

"The above-mentioned Governments and the French National Committee condemn in the strongest possible terms this bestial policy of cold-blooded extermination. They declare that such events can only strengthen the resolve of all freedom-loving people to overthrow the barbarous Hitlerite tyranny. They reaffirm their solemn resolution to ensure that those responsible for these

crimes shall not escape retribution and to press on
with the necessary practical measures to ensure
this end."

While the value of this Declaration is great, it would have
been preferable, the writer feels, if it had ended on another note. The Jewish People are not seeking retribution. They believe what God has said: "Vengeance is
Mine. I will repay." What they desire to hear is an answer
to the pertinent questions put by the Chief Rabbi of the
British Empire in his address on the special Day of Fast-
ing and Prayer observed by the Jews of Great Britain on
13th December. "What are the United Nations prepared
to do?" asked Dr. Hertz. "Will they, among other things
open the gates of their countries to those few who, as if
by a miracle, escape from the Nazi inferno? Will Britain
and her Allies encourage and help the few remaining
neutral States to receive such refugees? Will at least the
children be saved from mass poisoning in the lethal
chambers of Hitler, from being buried alive in thousands
by his hell-hounds? Shame covers us, as Jews, as Eng-
lishmen, as Human Beings, that even to this question we
are not sure of an affirmative answer."

www.ingramcontent.com/pod-product-compliance
Lightning Source LLC
Chambersburg PA
CBHW020534290526
45786CB00002B/872